HOW TO START YOUR OWN
MAGAZINE

HOW TO START YOUR OWN
MAGAZINE

W. P. Williams and Joseph Van Zandt

cbi **Contemporary Books, Inc.**
Chicago

Library of Congress Cataloging in Publication Data

Williams, W. P., 1953-
   How to start your own magazine.

   Includes index.
   1. Periodicals, Publishing of. I. Van Zandt, Joseph,
1940-   joint author.   II. Title.
Z286.P4W54   658.8'09'070572   78-57480
ISBN 0-8092-7444-2
ISBN 0-8092-7443-4-pbk.

Copyright © 1978 by W. P. Williams and Joseph Van Zandt
All rights reserved
Published by Contemporary Books, Inc.
180 North Michigan Avenue, Chicago, Illinois 60601
Manufactured in the United States of America
Library of Congress Catalog Card Number: 78-57480
International Standard Book Number: 0-8092-7444-2 (cloth)
                                    0-8092-7443-4 (paper)

Published simultaneously in Canada by
Beaverbooks
953 Dillingham Road
Pickering, Ontario L1W 1Z7
Canada

Contents

Introduction	vii
1. Do you really want to start a magazine?	1
2. Picking a field of interest and raising money	5
3. Layout and content	17
4. Production	37
5. Printing your magazine	53
6. Holding costs down	59

7. Building circulation	69
8. Promotion is important, too	75
9. How to sell ad space	79
10. Odds and ends	95
Glossary of publishing terms	105
Index	109

Introduction

When it comes to career fantasies, probably no other position offers the glamour and prestige of a magazine publisher. In movies and on television shows, magazine publishers and editors are shown moving in the same circles as prominent business leaders, politicians, and celebrities. And through the articles in their publications, these magazine moguls influence public opinion and the course of human events.

How many times have you thought of a terrific idea for a new magazine while daydreaming on the commuter train or in the car, but then dismissed the idea because it seemed too fantastic and impossible to realize? It takes years of experience and big bucks, right? Then, five or six months later, you spotted *your* magazine idea right there on the rack—someone else obviously thought it was a good scheme, too, but he or she *acted* on the belief.

The surprising fact is that just about anyone with a reasonable amount of intelligence and time can become a magazine publisher. What may surprise you even more is that the little guy often has a greater chance of success than the big guy in this continually expanding field.

Introduction   viii

How to Start Your Own Magazine explains why you might want to publish your own magazine and then provides you with a step-by-step plan for turning your concept into a viable, dynamic business. And if you are short on cash, don't worry—authors W. P. Williams and Joseph Van Zandt, both successful magazine publishers and free-lance writers, tell you how to break down finanical barriers and get the money men eating out of your hand.

Man or woman, young or old, if you would like to turn your dreams into reality, this book will show you how, with chapters on everything from creating a format to building circulation. Williams and Van Zandt will tell you how to fill your pages with articles from top authors and journalists at little or no cost to you; how to arrange for retail distribution and maneuver your magazine to the front of the racks; and how to get free publicity for your magazine in newspapers and on radio and television shows.

If you would really like to become a publishing magnate, on a small or grand scale, this book will show you how to do it today.

1
Do you really want to start a magazine?

That's an odd thing to ask at the very beginning of a book designed to show you how to start your own magazine. But the question must be asked. After all, isn't it better to check your motives and commitment now, rather than invest many months of hard work and perhaps a good deal of money only to discover you should have opened a greenhouse?

Exactly why do you think you'd like to be the publisher, and perhaps the editor as well, of your own magazine? An obvious answer is money. You believe that the publishing field offers the best chance for large returns with limited investment. After all, if Hefner could turn a $500 loan into a multimillion-dollar empire, why not you? Well, let's be realistic. The odds of duplicating the *Playboy* success story are about equal to winning the Irish Sweepstakes. Nonetheless, that doesn't mean that you don't have a good shot at succeeding on a smaller scale.

Another valid reason for wanting to start your own magazine is the desire to obtain the means for influencing large numbers of people. You've probably heard the old bromide "the pen is mightier than the sword," and to a certain extent it is true. But there is another old saying that "power corrupts, and absolute power corrupts absolutely."

No matter what kind of noble motives you may attribute to your desire to wield the pen, in plain English you seek power. And despite all the virtues attributed to the Fourth Estate, any publisher (and most editors) will admit that the hard realities of the profession require him or her to negotiate, to compromise, and to accommodate.

The cub reporter and the neophyte free-lance writer come out of journalism school ready to cure all the world's ills through their hard-nosed investigating and impartial reporting. What they fail to realize is that Watergate-type scandals are broken only a few times in a generation. Even full-time investigative reporters such as Woodward and Bernstein usually stumble onto journalistic bombshells through an incredible series of lucky breaks.

Most people also fail to realize that even crusading newspapers and magazines have some sacred cows—to be "attacked" only in severe circumstances. Police all have their sources of information in the underworld, and they protect these sources in order to get at other, more evil types. Likewise, the experienced journalist has his own sources which he protects.

Reporters often hold a hot story at the request of police and in return get favors, such as hot tips and inside information for future stories. Publishers will stretch a deadline, or remake several pages to get a major advertiser's ad into a favored spot in the magazine or newspaper. An editor may decide, because the mayor is a good news source, to kill a story that the mayor's daughter got a speeding ticket.

Granted, you'll never hear about these kinds of "procedures" in journalism school, and if you go strictly by the book, they are taboo. But to launch a new magazine with the idea of living up to all the lofty ideals you've witnessed in textbooks and movies with absolutely no flexibility is to invite disaster.

We're not suggesting that you become totally pragmatic and throw ethics to the wind, because this course also will be destructive. What you must learn is to treat every case individually: to be tough when your instincts tell you to, and to bend a

Do you really want to start a magazine? 3

little when that course makes the most sense. Remember, the power of the press can corrupt the rigidly self-righteous as well as the total pragmatist. Steer a middle road and you will be least likely to succumb.

So, we've covered two basic attractions of publishing—money and power. But if you really want just money and power, you'll be better off going into politics, or organizing your own religion.

In our opinion, there are a lot of other attractive reasons for publishing your own magazine, and they are at least as valid as the first two:

• Publishing your own magazine can be a great deal of fun, despite frequently long hours, crises of all kinds, and occasional shortages of ready cash.

• You meet a wide variety of interesting people, regardless of the field you cover.

• You often get to do a lot of traveling, and in many cases, you can combine business and pleasure with the whole shot tax-deductible.

• Few enterprises can offer the same kind of ego gratification as that experienced when each new issue comes off the press bearing your own special imprimatur and your name on top of the masthead.

• Editors and publishers are in one of the most envied professions. Others, including top executives and successful entrepreneurs in other fields, see publishing as a glamorous, exciting, adventurous pursuit, even if your magazine happens to be devoted to as pedestrian a subject as stamp collecting.

• Press credentials can open all kinds of doors that are closed to mere mortals, from entrance to the press box at a hockey game, to admission to the press gallery of the state legislature or other governing body.

• Once you get your magazine on track and work out the kinks, you will find that you can often take several days or even a week off between issues for some fishing or fun in the sun. And if you publish a seasonal magazine, you may even have several months in the off-season when you can literally close shop.

• Whether your magazine business is operated as a proprietorship, a partnership, or a corporation, it will provide you with a wide variety of tax loopholes and other fringe benefits, from car and expense account to medical and retirement programs.

Okay; so now that you've taken a look at all the potential benefits of going into the publishing game, you're sold, right? But don't forget, there are two sides to the coin. At the risk of frightening you off, we'll give you some other things to consider:

• Your chances of success will be greatly magnified if you have at least some sort of background in publishing, whether it be as a writer, a photographer, an ad salesman, or a circulation man. Obviously, the broader your experience, the better your chances. Starting a magazine with absolutely no experience in the field can be compared to starting a restaurant or an auto body shop with no experience—yes, you still can succeed, but your chances will certainly be diminished. The best way to counter the odds is by hiring one or more real pros for your staff.

• Magazines, both consumer and trade, are highly subject to the whims of economic conditions. In a recession, the first things to suffer are "discretionary funds," whether they be a housewife's "mad money" or the ad budget of a major corporation. That means your ad revenues as well as your subscription and retail sales revenues can be hurt by circumstances beyond your control.

• Many of your operating costs, including the ever-increasing cost of paper and postage, are also beyond your control. Every publisher cringes when he is forced to announce even a modest rate hike, even when his own costs are soaring.

• You might start a magazine which is all alone in its field, only to see competitors pop up overnight, sometimes with the backing of major corporations.

• New publishers must rely almost entirely on outside typesetters, lithographers, printers, and mailing houses to get their product out. You could be at the mercy of people who may not share your concern for holding down costs or meeting deadlines.

If after weighing the pros and cons, you are still excited about starting your own magazine, you are ready for the next step—raising money to finance your venture.

2
Picking a field of interest and raising money

The biggest stumbling block to starting your magazine, or any business for that matter, is money. Most would-be entrepreneurs never do anything more than dream about their business ideas because (a) they think it will take much more money to start the business than is really the case, and (b) they don't think they will be able to borrow that amount or raise it through investors.

The facts speak otherwise. In the publishing field, success stories abound. Lloyd Hollister borrowed $50 to publish the first edition of the *Winnetka Talk* back in the Depression, and in 1972 he sold what had become a chain of ten weeklies, with a combined circulation in excess of 90,000, to Time, Inc. for a reported $5.5 million.

The Reader, an alternative free weekly paper, was started in an attic on the North Side of Chicago a few years ago, and today that paper employs a score of people and has grown from 16 to more than 100 pages, much of it advertising matter.

Joe Van Zandt and Wendy Williams, the co-authors of this book, started *Skisport* magazine five years ago with virtually no capital, and today it and its sister publication, the *Annual Skisport Vacation Guide*, gross close to $100,000 annually in revenue from ads, subscriptions, and newsstand sales.

Such stories could also be told of publications which fold each year, because many do. But the point is that it is possible to start a magazine or newspaper or journal without massive financial backing and make it a success. In fact, a survey of those publications which have folded in recent years as well as those which have prospered will provide the key to your own success.

Most of the publications which went under were general-interest periodicals, with national distribution and heavy financial backing. A perfect case in point is *Life* magazine, a picture periodical which listed many of the nation's finest photo-journalists on its staff, and which had a long and proud history of journalistic achievements. It was finally put to rest because it had outlived its value with the coming of television.

Metropolitan daily newspapers are another endangered species in the publishing field. Hardly a year goes by that at least half a dozen large newspapers don't sign "30" to their final edition. In 1970, for example, Chicago had four daily newspapers, ranging in circulation from 400,000 to almost 1,000,000. In 1973, *Chicago Today* was axed by its parent Tribune Co., because of steadily declining circulation and advertising and steadily increasing costs. Then, in March of 1978, the *Chicago Daily News* wrote its own obituary for its last edition, headlined "So Long, Chicago." The demise of the paper which once listed such luminaries as Carl Sandburg and some 17 Pulitzer Prize winners on its staff could not be deterred, even though a multimillion-dollar circulation was launched in late 1977 by publisher Marshall Field V.

Step No. 1—Choosing the subject matter

Well, you ask, if giants of the industry such as these can't cut it in this day of instant communication, how can an amateur like me? The answer is simply that if you can fill a need for information not satisfied by radio and television or other already successful publications, you very definitely can succeed.

In the publishing field, such specialized magazines and journals are called vertical books. (*Book* is a synonym for any periodical, from daily newspapers to annuals and yearbooks.) And while the electronic media have shown their ability to roll right over big city daily newspapers and beat them to the punch with late-breaking stories, radio and TV can't begin to compete with other publications, whether they be the suburban weekly which reports local news from honor rolls to wedding announcements, the monthly magazine of a hot new disco, or a newsletter for those interested in speculating in grain futures.

In other words, a vertical publication can be so designated because it is distributed in a limited geographic area, because it is distributed to a highly specialized group of people, or because it covers a single subject in great detail.

Examples of such magazines abound. In the sports field, there are magazines devoted exclusively to professional football, a few of which are limited further to a particular team, such as *Chicago Football Weekly*, which is essentially for Bears fans. In the field of skiing, more than a dozen regional ski magazines and newspapers prosper, even though there are two major national magazines. There is even a ski magazine devoted exclusively to cross-country skiers, another for powder hounds, and a third devoted to ski racing. In the boating field, literally scores of local, regional, and national publications abound, covering everything from canoeing to ocean yacht racing. The *Hobie Hot Line,* for example, is a slick monthly magazine which goes exclusively to owners of Hobie Cat sailboats. Other specialty magazines are written for chess players, for owners of hunting dogs, for skateboarders, for amateur craftsmen, and on practically ad infinitum.

Why do these publications succeed in such great numbers while the giants of general information fall all around them? Because they give their readers news, features, and photos of specialized subjects which they can't obtain anywhere else. And they give advertisers of products and services in the field a place to sell their wares without wasting a lot of money reaching people who have no interest in what they have to offer.

All you have to do is find a field of interest which has a reasonable size of following, either on a local, regional, or national basis, and which is not currently served by another publication, and half the battle is won.

When the women's liberation movement began, it didn't take long for related publications to appear—*Ms.* and *womenSports* among the better known. When hang gliding caught on, it was just a few months before the first issue of *Hang Gliding* magazine appeared. The skateboarding fad has resulted in several new magazines, as have the custom van phenomenon, the dirt bike boom, and even the new singles life-style.

So put your mind to work, preferably in an area in which you have an interest and more than a passing knowledge. How about a magazine for amateur astronomers? Or maybe a magazine just for owners of Afghan hounds? Or a magazine devoted to salmon fishing on the Great Lakes?

If you sit down and talk about it with a few friends, chances are that in an hour or less, you could come up with a list of at least a dozen possible topics for a magazine.

The next step is to determine which of these fields of interest already has a publication and whether there is room for another. One way is to make some phone calls or send letters to people who would be in a position to know of such publications. For example, suppose you live in the north central United States and you decide that the state of Wisconsin could use a publication for snowmobilers. Your first step might be to stop in at one or two snowmobile shops in your town to see if any regional magazines are being sold there. Ask the proprietor if he knows of any such magazines. If he says no, then write or call several snowmobile manufacturers, directing your inquiry to the advertising department. (After all, if such a publication does exist, chances are the ad people deal with it.)

Suppose everything is go up to this point. As a final precaution, get a recent copy of Standard Rate & Data Service's consumer magazine directory. It has up-to-date information (including ad rates) on literally thousands of magazines ranging

Picking a field of interest and raising money

in size from those with a circulation of 2,000 to 3,000 to major magazines such as *Sports Illustrated* and *Cosmopolitan*. It even lists new magazines which have filed for a listing but have not yet been accepted.

We've devoted the past several pages to the topic of subject matter or field of interest for your magazine. The reason is that a major factor in your ability to raise capital will be your ability to convince the lending institution or potential investor that your magazine will not have to compete with too many others in its field for ad revenue and reader support.

But don't get overanxious yet. You still have several projects to complete before you are ready to raise money.

Step No. 2—Lining up potential advertisers

While it is a fact that few publications are able to show a profit from the very first issue, you certainly want to keep losses to a minimum while you build advertiser support and paid circulation. The way to do this is to develop as much revenue as possible right from the word go.

A lot of companies and agencies will not advertise in untried publications—they want you to establish a track record first. But there are others that will spend ad dollars, even in your very first issue. Some automatically budget a small percentage of their advertising dollars to just such new magazines as yours, in the belief that they have a responsibility to do so. Others will see the potential in your idea and will want to establish a working relationship before you start growing, in the belief that as a charter advertiser, they will receive special treatment later.

Your first job is to develop an advertiser list, which includes as many potential advertisers AND their ad agencies as possible. Again, the way to start is by sitting down and listing every individual, company, and organization which might possibly advertise in a magazine such as yours.

Suppose you decide to produce a magazine for Great Lakes salmon fishermen. What sort of companies and individuals would you include in your advertiser list? Well, for starters, there are the scores of companies which make fishing tackle. Then, there are the manufacturers of boats and motors. Next, you could add the companies which manufacture other products in some way useful to fishermen; these could include, for example, special apparel and electronic aids (depth finders, radio direction finders, radar, and the like).

At this point, you will have a list of several hundred potential advertisers, and you've just scratched the surface. How about marinas, shorefront restaurants, and motels? How about organizations such as Salmon Unlimited? And don't forget the owners of the hundreds of charter boats which are available for hire by groups of fishermen.

Next, start developing a list of secondary potential advertisers, including tobacco and liquor companies, automobile companies (especially those which make special models of cars and trucks for towing boats), and other companies interested in reaching sportsmen with their product messages.

Look through magazines for possible additions to your advertiser list. Often, an ad will include a company's address and sometimes even its phone number. Be sure to copy that information down, because you will need it.

Getting the complete address and phone number and the names of key advertising people, as well as the addresses and names of key people at each company's ad agency, is a time-consuming chore, but there are ways to make it easier. First of all, go to your local library or write to Standard Rate & Data Service (5201 Old Orchard Road, Skokie, IL 60076, and get a copy of the SRDS Red Book of Advertising Agencies and the SRDS Advertiser Book. These will have most of the information you need, provided the company and/or agency is listed. If it isn't, or you need additional information, call or write in care of the ad department.

IMPORTANT: Before you send out a single inquiry, have some business stationery printed that includes your magazine name, address, and logo (insignia). If you don't have a business address, or at least a house with an address which sounds as if it could be a business address, get a post office box. Companies and ad agencies will almost always respond to a typed letter on official-looking letterhead. They will seldom respond to a letter on your own personal stationery or on plain paper.

Remember that your magazine is an unknown quantity at this point, so the only impression the company or agency will have is that provided by your letter. It had better look professional.

In composing your letter, don't go into great detail about the fact that yours is a brand-new magazine or any of that. It's better simply to state that you would like to add key names to your mailing list. Include a brief questionnaire at the bottom of your letter and enclose a stamped, addressed envelope (which also includes your logo and return address).

For those companies which fail to respond, get on the horn and ask for the information personally. In short, don't let a single stumbling block stop you.

Figure on spending anywhere from three to six months to develop a fairly thorough advertiser list, especially if you are developing it just in your spare time, while working another job.

The obvious reason for developing an advertiser list is so that you can send them your sales materials and eventually make calls. But you can also use your list to determine whether or not your idea for a new magazine appeals to the people you will be relying on for ad revenue.

There are many ways to accomplish this:

One is to prepare a questionnaire, briefly explaining the concept of the new magazine and asking the ad managers and agency people to answer such questions as: Do they feel the idea is a good one? Why? What should the editorial material include? How often should it be published? Should the format be standard magazine or tabloid? Most important of all, ask whether they would support such a magazine. If a fairly significant number of respondents say yes, then not only do you have a priority list of contacts, but you also can include the letters as part of your pro forma, or detailed business plan. Such responses are guaranteed to influence bankers and investors positively.

A better way of winning advertiser support before you produce your first regular issue is to make a mock-up, or pilot issue, with enough pages to give an idea of the look of the real magazine. Have enough printed for everyone on your mailing list and send each one out with accompanying questionnaire and/or ad contract. You will be surprised to find that some of the respondents will actually send back a signed contract, which impresses bankers and investors even more.

Consider offering as an incentive, a special discount from your regular rates for advertisers who make a commitment before a certain date. Even better, offer a greater discount for those who make a commitment for several succeeding issues. (How to determine ad rates and prepare a rate card will be discussed later.) This approach will give you the most "ammunition" for your pro forma, which, in turn, will give you the best shot at borrowing the money you need.

But to go the pilot issue route, you must have several thousand dollars to invest BEFORE you go to the bank for the big wad—that is, unless you are able to persuade a printer to extend credit on the strength of your idea. Fortunately, it is a buyer's market right now in the printing industry, which means the chances of obtaining credit for printing your pilot issue are pretty good.

Step No. 3—Preparing the pro forma

A pro forma is a document which is presented to your banker and/or investors to show graphically the potential for your magazine.

A pro forma is like a job résumé, except that it deals with future plans instead of past accomplishments, and it should be much more detailed and documented—in fact, your own job résumé should be a part of it, especially if your career relates to the new magazine in some way.

The pro forma should include a description of the magazine, including format, content, scope of circulation, and frequency of publication. If you will face competing magazines, explain why your magazine will succeed. If you will have the field to yourself, be sure to stress this point. Next, your pro forma should include a detailed list of advertisers, stating the type of commitment each has made. Signed contracts or questionnaires should be available as proof of your claims. Finally, your pro forma should include a detailed list of anticipated expenses for a full year of operation and a detailed breakdown of anticipated revenues from ad sales, newsstand sales, and subscriptions.

If you determine that you will need $50,000 or less, and you are fairly adept at figures, you can probably prepare your own pro forma. If you need more money, you would be wise to see a certified public accountant for help in preparing the pro forma. And if you are really going for a bundle, consider hiring a firm which specializes in preparing pro formas and assisting new companies in raising capital.

But here again, as in preparing a pilot issue, you'll need at least some of your own money to get the ball rolling. (Figure $7,000 or so to have a pro forma prepared for a loan of $1 million or more.)

How detailed should your pro forma be? For a loan in the $25,000-to-$50,000 range, a pro forma of five or six pages, including financial figures, should be sufficient. For a king-sized loan, your pro forma can run to 50 pages or more.

Step No. 4—Presenting your case

Preparing a detailed, comprehensive business plan is essential to borrowing the money required to launch your new magazine. But it is only half the battle. The other half must be won by you personally, in the way you present your case to a banker or potential investor.

Unless you plan to start a major nationally circulated magazine, you will be better off borrowing the money on your own. After all, why cut in a group of silent partners if you can keep the whole pie for yourself?

If you are worried about taking the risk on your own, maybe you aren't ready for going into business. And your fears will certainly show when you talk to your banker.

The preparation of your pro forma, plus discussions you will have with businessmen, potential advertisers, and others during the months it takes to get everything together, will prepare you for the final test—talking to your banker and/or investors.

If you decide to go the direct route and borrow all you need from a bank or other lending institution, don't go just to the closest one, or even the one where you have been doing your personal banking. Ask around, talk with local businessmen, with other entrepreneurs, and with your lawyer and accountant, to determine which banks in your area have the most forward-thinking personnel and liberal loan policies. Go to them first.

Using your magazine's letterhead, send the president of the bank a brief letter explaining that you would like to arrange a meeting to discuss a business loan. Mention one or two of the more impressive statistics from your pro forma and tell him you will telephone for an appointment in a few days. (This will show him you are sure of yourself.)

When you call, the president may decide to talk to you himself. Or he may turn you over to a vice-president in charge of business loans. Either way, you win, because either you talk to the top man who has the authority to approve most loans by himself, or you talk to the second in command who figures you have clout with the boss because he referred you.

Once the appointment is made, drop your pro forma off at the bank with a brief note explaining that you felt it would be helpful if the officer had the opportunity to study the pro forma in advance.

Now, when you do go in, chances are the banker will have a lot of questions for you, which you can routinely answer instead of conducting a formal presentation.

If you aren't already dealing with the bank, make a commitment to establish your business account there, and to switch any personal accounts as well. It won't hurt to mention that in the future, after your magazine is off and rolling, you intend to make additional loans as needed for equipment purchases and expansion. This will make points both for the potential business you are offering, and for the obvious confidence you have in your project.

Never, in the course of discussion, should you be anything but firmly positive. Avoid using words such as "if" and "we hope." Always phrase your sentences as statements of fact: "After we achieve our initial objective for circulation, we will then launch an intensive direct mail campaign to boost paid circulation to the 50,000 mark."

You could get your money during that first meeting. Or the banker may have to present the request to a loan committee, depending on the amount and the bank's policy, so don't get discouraged if you are put off. As long as the answer isn't a firm "no," you are still in the running.

Don't try another bank until you are sure that the first has turned you down. Bankers have a way of talking about interesting prospects and you could blow the whole deal if you move too fast; no banker will lend you money if he thinks you are making promises to him and then dealing with his competitors at the same time.

If you *are* turned down, ask for specific reasons why. Then adjust your pro forma (and, if necessary, your entire concept) before approaching another bank. This way, you will boost your chances by erasing any negatives in advance.

So much for dealing with banks. What if you elect to form a corporation and then sell stock to investors? First of all, keep at least 51 percent for yourself and sell only enough stock to raise the required money.

Then, if you need more capital at a later date, you can either sell some more of your own stock or go to a bank for a loan, this time as a viable, functioning corporation.

Where do you find investors? Your first thought is probably family and friends, but these are the last people you should consider. If the business fails, you'll have a lot of angry friends and relatives who will expect you to make good on their loans. If the magazine succeeds, you'll have all kinds of suggestions coming your way from people it may be difficult to say "no" to.

One method of attracting investors is to advertise in local newspapers, either in the classified section or on the business pages. Another way is to contact a broker who specializes in getting investors together with entrepreneurs.

The final method is to send letters to well-to-do people in your community, briefly explaining your idea and offering to meet with them if they are interested in learning more. This is a hit-or-miss approach, but if you contact enough people, a certain percent will definitely contact you. And if you sell them on your idea, chances are excellent that they in turn will get some of their own wealthy friends to invest.

Do not approach a major magazine publisher with your idea. If it is good, you may find yourself aced out by an unscrupulous publisher. At best, the publishing company will demand control of the company, and may very well ease you out after the magazine is off the ground.

If your magazine concept is one which lends itself to promotion of a particular product or service, you may be able to get a corporation to back you.

In any case, the capital is out there. All you have to do is map a logical plan to get what funds you need.

3
Layout and content

You need both solid content and layout to ensure your magazine's success. And, yes, that does include your ads—you would be surprised at how many of your readers buy your magazines at least in part because the ads are helpful to them in their business, hobby, or area of special interest.

Content

The content of your magazine will depend on the parameters you set when you first decide what area of interest you will deal with. But regardless of whether it is astrology or agriculture, the general categories of editorial material will be pretty much the same.

First, there are the hard news stories, which deal strictly in fact and are reported in a simple and straightforward manner. Next come the many and various types of feature articles—some which take an offbeat approach to a current news topic, and others which delve into an unusual or unique topic.

News and features are the bread and butter of magazines as

well as newspapers, although magazines generally lean heavily on the feature approach, in stories and photos as well as layout. But there are other categories of editorial material which you may decide to include as a regular part of your content.

For example, there is the editorial, usually placed on a specially designated page, and expressing the official view of the management (which essentially means you). Then there are interpretive articles, in which the writer or reporter mixes opinion, conjecture, and speculation with the hard facts (those which are substantiated).

Then there are the various regular columns which appear in many magazines. Sometimes, these columns are always written by a specific author and carry simply his or her name in what is called a "standing head." (That means it remains the same from issue to issue.) Other columns may be written by a different writer each time, or may be a compilation of contributions by several people. Contents of such columns are determined by subject matter: People and Places, Information for Buyers, Personnel Changes, Calendar of Events, and so on.

Other forms of editorial content might include the literary essay, letters to the editor, a technical Q & A (question and answer) column, photo layout (with or without accompanying copy block), and perhaps something brand-new and invented by you for a specific purpose.

Determining what kinds of editorial material belong in your magazine need not be done all at once. One of the keys to a successful magazine is its ability to change and adapt to new requirements of readers and advertisers. So don't be afraid to experiment. If an idea bombs, drop it.

Don't hesitate to study closely the successful magazines in all fields. In fact, make a point of it. And don't be afraid to use an idea you think might work for you. Top magazines keep a close watch on each other, and when a hot idea appears in one, it usually isn't long before it shows up in other publications.

For example, when *People* magazine proved an overnight success, imitators began cropping up. Even the tawdry national tabloids began to lean more toward light "people" items and less on stories of UFOs, gruesome murders, and bizarre sexual tales.

And the major metropolitan daily papers got into the act with new and better gossip columns and stories.

Once you determine the kind of pieces and columns which will compose your editorial product, you must decide the best AND most economical method of filling these needs.

Sure, stories by the likes of Truman Capote and Norman Mailer might give you instant prestige, but can you really afford the talents of writers such as these? Often, lesser-known writers can fill your needs just as well, and for a fraction of the cost.

If you are dealing with technical subjects, be sure to use writers who really understand them. But be careful about letting experts in the field write articles or columns unless they are also proven writers. And be sure to spell out in no uncertain terms that you and your staff are the editors. You will have final say on what goes into print and what doesn't. If a story must be trimmed, you will do it.

Any other policy will have the experts driving you crazy with complaints, last-minute changes, and "suggestions" on everything from how to crop photos to the size type you select for their articles.

Since you bought this book to help you launch your own magazine, chances are pretty good that you are a writer already—a working journalist, a part-time free-lancer, an ad copywriter, a public relations man, or maybe even an amateur whose material has yet to be published.

In any case, you'll be a step ahead if you are able to handle at least some of the writing chores for your magazine yourself. There are things which must be written for each issue, and often at the last minute—captions for photos, editor's notes and special introductions to articles, answers to letters to the editor, not to mention additions and insertions you feel are necessary in articles. Occasionally an entire article will have to be written because it was somehow forgotten when the assignments were made.

If you are unable to take on these kinds of writing chores, it doesn't mean you can't publish a magazine. But it will require that you hire a full-time, experienced editor. If you wish to retain the title of editor and publisher, call your working editor "managing editor" or "executive editor." As editor in chief, you will be able to participate in long-range planning and direction while leaving the day-to-day operations to your full-time professional.

A top pro will cost you $30,000 or more in salary. A competent but non-stellar editor will cost $20,000 or so. If you go for the bargain basement, you'll get either an old-timer who is over the hill and probably burned out, a person with a serious problem such as alcoholism, or else a green kid just out of college.

Of the three, we'd opt for the green kid if we were unable to afford a real pro. There is an overabundance of young people coming out of journalism schools these days, and through careful screening, you could land someone with loads of talent for as little as $12,000.

Of course, chances are he or she will stick around just for a year or two, using your magazine as a stepping-stone. Then you'll have to scramble to find a replacement so there will be no interruption in your operation.

If you elect to function as your own managing editor, keep in mind that you will also have to deal with all the various publishing functions as well. Most of the editor-publishers we know admit that they spend far less time than they would like on the editorial product—sometimes as few as four or five working days a month.

And here is where one of the basic truths of the publishing game hits home. You must learn to compromise, to accept less than perfection, and to roll with the punches if you intend to avoid ulcers, heart attacks, and sheer exhaustion in getting each issue out.

A longtime friend of ours who has been producing magazines for years put it succinctly: "You do the best you can in the time allowed; then you wrap it up and move on to the next issue. Don't second-guess yourself, and never look back."

What he was saying, in effect, is that magazines are like newspapers. They operate on a tight and inflexible schedule. All deadlines—editorial, advertising, and production—must be sacred.

Layout and content 21

As an independent magazine publisher, you will almost certainly have your product printed at an outside printing plant. You will also probably use outside firms for such things as typesetting, pasteup, and processing of photos into halftone negatives or screened Photostats. At least, this will be the case until you become established and learn the ropes. Then you can begin moving various steps in the actual production of your magazine from an outside to an in-house operation. (We'll discuss this in greater detail in the chapter on production and printing.)

The point we're getting to is this: since you will be relying in large part on outside suppliers and companies for putting your magazine together and printing it, you must be able to give these companies a long-range production schedule, outlining what you need from each and when you need it. They in turn must be able to work your magazine into their own schedules.

For example, suppose you are planning to produce your May issue. You want it off the presses and in the hands of your mailing house and retail distributors in time to reach the magazine racks by April 15 (almost all successful magazines reach retail outlets two weeks before the date on the cover of the issue).

Your mailing house and distributors say they need seven to ten days to process your magazines and move them. So you know that you must be off the presses by April 5 at the latest.

Your printing house tells you it needs ten working days to shoot your pasted-up pages into full-page negatives and to strip them up and add halftones before making plates for the presses. So that means your finished pages must reach the printing plant by March 22 or thereabouts depending on where the weekends fall.

Let's assume that your typesetter is capable of pasting up your pages, which is done on the basis of your layouts. He requires a full working week to set your type and another week for pasteup, including making changes that may be dictated when a layout dummy, a blueprint, or a schematic drawing doesn't work out as intended.

Now you are all the way back to March 8 as the deadline for

getting all editorial material and dummies to the typesetter. You and your staffers will also require time to lay out, or "dummy out," the issue, including writing headlines, putting ads in place, and so on. Assuming you are able to complete these tasks in a week, and allowing another week for editing the various articles and columns planned for this issue, your final deadline for submission of editorial and ad material is somewhere around February 23 for your May issue.

To the uninitiated, this seems an incredible length of time—roughly eight weeks—but to those with any kind of experience with magazines, this schedule is actually extremely tight, and it doesn't even allow for complications. Nonetheless, it does serve to point up two very important considerations: deadlines and advance planning.

Deadlines

Deadlines must be considered absolutely sacred. If a single date in your schedule of deadlines is missed, it will throw the entire series out of sync. And since every one of your suppliers is dealing with scores of other publishers, some or all of them must do a juggling act of their own to try to bail you out.

If they are able to rescue you, it will cost you plenty in overtime hours and penalty charges. If they can't, the next outside supplier down the line is suddenly hit, and so on until you get to the printing plant. Miss your final deadline and you may not be able to get your magazine rescheduled and on the presses for days or weeks.

And don't bother threatening. At this point, the printer is definitely in the driver's seat. He is not about to bump all of his other customers back to make room for you after you missed your deadline and cost him plenty in press downtime and lost man-hours.

Assuming you have missed a press date and as a result got your product out a week late, you now have an angry mailing house and angry distributors. Your magazines reach subscribers, advertisers, and potential advertisers late. They go on the newsstands long after the competition does, and sales slump as a result.

Some of your advertisers will be upset. Some may refuse to pay for an ad which failed to announce a sale or special deal in time. Others may demand discounts because of the likelihood of reaching fewer readers than promised. Some agencies may even cancel their ad contracts since you have put them behind the eight ball after they recommended your magazine to their clients.

The net result will be extremely costly in loss of current and potential ad revenue, in reduced retail sales, in increased production costs, and in angry suppliers. And all this is a result of missing your deadlines for a single issue. Miss deadlines for several issues, and you won't have to worry any more—you'll be out of business.

Advance planning

Since, as we have shown, there is usually a minimum of 10 weeks' time between editorial deadlines and publication date for a given issue of your magazine, and usually more like 15 or 20 weeks' lead time, advance planning is an absolute must.

Just as clothing stores buy spring clothes the previous summer and put them on sale as early as January, the magazine publisher must be thinking about winter stories in the spring and about summer stories in the fall.

Smart editors and publishers will plan specific issues as far as a year in advance. They leave openings for hot items and stories dealing with late-breaking developments in a given field, but for as many articles and columns as possible, they try to anticipate.

Ever wonder how a magazine which comes in November can have an article on skiing at Aspen, or spending Christmas in the Bahamas? The articles were assigned the previous fall so the writers and photographers could visit the places and gather material the previous winter.

An added benefit of preparing story schedules a year in advance is that you can then use the schedule as a sales tool.

You might include a story schedule in your media kit (packet of materials which is sent to potential advertisers and their agencies).

If you are planning a special issue on a particular subject, you can now point this out to specific advertisers. For example, suppose you publish a magazine on arts and crafts and you are planning a special issue dealing with the annual arts and crafts show in New York. You advise your advertisers about this issue. Perhaps you will print several thousand additional copies for distribution at the show. Perhaps you will have a special discount for advertisers in this issue. You tell this to the advertiser to help him make up his mind on advertising.

More on content

In mapping editorial plans, be sure to look back over your schedules for previous years (assuming, of course, that you are still in business after several years). Try to avoid redoing the same old hackneyed stories. Avoid the same old approaches year after year. Repetition of editorial content is one sure way to prematurely kill a magazine.

Be sure, also, to keep close tabs on any competitors in the field as well as noncompetitive magazines which may occasionally run articles in your area of interest, or "editorial territory." If you elect to write about a given person or subject which has recently been done by another publication, make every effort to ensure that your piece takes a fresh approach and also includes new information.

Layout

Magazine layout is an exact science, requiring a mathematical mind and a knowledge of printers' terminology and limitations.

Magazine layout is also an art. It takes an appreciation of spatial relations between various forms and shapes, plus the ability to see in your mind's eye how a layout will look when it is transformed from a dummy sheet to finished page.

Good layout editors are a lot like top athletes: they achieve great things, but they can't always say how they did it. Ask Reggie Jackson how he hit those three home runs in a single World Series game and he probably couldn't tell you. At least he couldn't give you a detailed description of what he was thinking and what each part of his body was doing as those three pitches came down the tube. Likewise, a good layout editor probably can't tell you exactly why he chose to scale a photo a certain way to go with a story, or why he chose 10-point Helvetica for the body type and 36-point Cooper Black for headline, with an 18-point "outquote" in the middle of the copy block.

Sure, there are all kinds of arbitrary rules of typography and layout, but the good editor knows that none are sacred. A few years ago, so-called "horizontal makeup" was very much in vogue for both newspapers and magazines. Stories were stretched across the page, with long, single-line headlines and with the result being a horizontal rectangle of type. Today, the horizontal concept has largely been replaced by what editors call "modular layout." Articles and photos are treated as a unit, again placed in rectangles on the page, but with a mix of horizontal and vertical units.

But the really sharp layout editor doesn't let himself get trapped into such boxes. He prefers to let each page come together on its own, and he doesn't hesitate to disregard sacred cows of layout. His guiding principle is simply to keep his layouts in tune with the personality of his publication while making sure that he adds to the reader's aesthetic pleasure.

In general, magazines devoted to business or science look best when their appearance is uncluttered. The use of sans serif headline and body type, of large graphs and charts when called for, and of crisp and clean layouts seems to work best. On the other hand, alternative magazines, such as those devoted to rock music, or to teen-age interests, or to controversial social issues, may require a much more vibrant (even frenetic) appearance to help convey their message. Such magazines may occasionally use vulgar language or photos for shock value. They may use elaborate, often garish, illustrations to rivet your attention. They often use bold splashes of color, vast amounts of white space, and other gimmicks. But as long as the result fits the personality of the magazine, we say bravo.

In Chapter 2, we alluded to the demise of the *Chicago Daily News* and an 11th-hour circulation drive which failed. Another desperate move by the *Daily News* was a complete change in appearance in the months before it folded. The traditional newspaper look was dropped in favor of avant-garde typefaces, bold column and cutoff rules, and layouts a la *Rolling Stone* magazine. Unfortunately, the new look was not accompanied by a similar bold shift in editorial content. Under its hip new appearance was the same old *Daily News,* complete with traditionally written news stories and pedantic editorials. Young singles and marrieds bought the new *Daily News* a few times because they were attracted by its new look. But they soon realized it was still the old *News* in disguise, and they stopped buying again. The paper died soon afterward.

The moral of this tale is simply that the content of your publication must be in tune with its graphics.

How your magazine should look will depend on a number of factors. There is no exactly correct look, and ten top layout people might come up with ten different-looking products if given a free hand to create what they think is the right look for your magazine. But although different, chances are that all ten will bear a certain resemblance to one another in both typography and layouts.

So, there can be any number of acceptable designs for your magazine. Likewise, there are unlimited numbers of incorrect designs. If you are unsure of yourself in this area, you would be better off to spend some money for the advice of a recognized expert.

Format

Basically, magazines are found in three formats. One is called the digest size, in obvious reference to the *Reader's Digest.* Dimensions are usually 5½ inches wide by 8½ inches deep (trim size).

The second and most popular format is the so-called standard magazine format. The trim size of its pages is 8½ inches wide by 11 inches deep (same as a sheet of business stationery) with the "live matter" running 7½ by 10 inches deep. ("Live matter" refers to type and photos which do not bleed, or run, off the page.) More than 90 percent of all magazines published today fit this format.

Finally, there is the tabloid format. Usually, tabloids are 11½ inches wide by 14 inches deep (trim size), although "tabs" can vary widely in both width and length of page, depending on the size of the rolls of paper used by the presses. *Rolling Stone*, for example, has a trim size of 11½ by 13 inches.

Your choice of format will depend on the kind of personality you want to create, as well as the amount of money you can afford to spend. We suggest you limit yourself to one of the three basic sizes.

Why? First of all, most ad agencies design their ad material to conform to these three basic sizes. Hit them with an oddball or "bastard" size page, and as often as not, you won't get their business.

Second, and equally important, most printing plants are set up for handling one or more of the three basic formats. You may elect to go with a bastard size because a certain plant gives you a terrific price, or because you want your magazine to stand out from the rest. But should that plant shut down, or raise its prices prohibitively, or start giving you poor quality copies, you will have to change printers. Suddenly, you will find your oddball format severely limits you in your choices.

We advise staying away from the digest size because not only does it limit the creativity of your layout editor, but it also is not nearly as popular with advertisers; they often feel they can't get their message across on such a small page.

If you want to produce a first-class publication, with a lot of use of color and high-quality reproduction of photos, your obvious choice is the standard magazine format. You will have a wide choice of printers, a page size which is most popular with advertisers, and enough room to produce attractive layouts.

What about the tabloid format? It is the first choice of those who want to convey a breezy, informal, and "with it" impression. The tabloid is also the obvious choice for those who want to keep their printing costs to a minimum. This may seem like a contradiction, since the tabloid page is the largest of the three popular sizes, but you should be advised that most tabloids are printed on newsprint (the kind of paper used in most newspapers) instead of the more costly coated and offset grades of paper. Tabloids are printed on high-speed offset web presses, which are designed to produce maximum quantities for minimum cost. Of course, quality does suffer as a result, but good web printers can still produce very good quality publications, as is evidenced by such nationally circulated tabloids as *Rolling Stone, CountryStyle,* and others.

Some well-known business publications, such as *Advertising Age,* use the tabloid format to convey the immediacy of a newspaper, but they print on expensive coated stock which is stitched and trimmed just like major magazines to assure their readers that their product is definitely first-class.

So when it comes to format, "you pay your money and you take your choice."

Typography

Typography refers to the many styles and sizes of type which are available. It is impossible to pinpoint the exact number of typefaces which are available at any given time, because new ones are being designed by the major type companies all the time, while older ones are being phased out. Suffice it to say that there are probably upwards of 2,000 typefaces available in sizes from 6 point (1/12 of an inch tall) to 144 point (2 inches tall), plus others both smaller and larger than the standard maximum and minimum sizes.

Selecting which typefaces will complement your magazine's personality is obviously not an easy task. However, you can reduce your choices immensely by limiting your selection to the half dozen or so most popular typefaces in both serif and sans serif faces.

Souvenir Light

6 point
ABCDEFGHIJKLMNOPQRSTUVWXYZ abcdefghijklmnopqrstuvwxyz 1234567890

8 point
ABCDEFGHIJKLMNOPQRSTUVWXYZ abcdefghijklmnopqrstuvwxyz 1234567890

9 point
ABCDEFGHIJKLMNOPQRSTUVWXYZ abcdefghijklmnopqrstuvwxyz 1234567890

10 point
ABCDEFGHIJKLMNOPQRSTUVWXYZ abcdefghijklmnopqrstuvwxyz 1234567890

12 point
ABCDEFGHIJKLMNOPQRSTUVWXYZ abcdefghijklmnopqrstuvwxyz

14 point
ABCDEFGHIJKLMNOPQRSTUVWXYZ abcdefghijklmnopqrstuv

18 point
ABCDEFGHIJKLMNOPQRSTUVWXYZ
abcdefghijklmnopqrstuvwxyz 1234567890

24 point
ABCDEFGHIJKLMNOPQRSTUVWX
abcdefghijklmnopqrstuvwxyz 1234567

30 point
ABCDEFGHIJKLMNOPQRS
abcdefghijklmnopqrstuvwxyz 1

36 point
ABCDEFGHIJKLMNOP
abcdefghijklmnopqrstuvw

Chart of Serif type

Avant Garde Gothic Book

6 point
Abcdefghijklmnopqrstuvwxyz abcdefghijklmnopqrstuvwxyz 1234567890

8 point
ABCDEFGHIJKLMNOPQRSTUVWXYZ abcdefghijklmnopqrstuvwxyz 1234567890

9 point
ABCDEFGHIJKLMNOPQRSTUVWXYZ abcdefghijklmnopqrstuvwxyz 1234567890

10 point
ABCDEFGHIJKLMNOPQRSTUVWXYZ abcdefghijklmnopqrstuvwxyz 1234567890

12 point
ABCDEFGHIJKLMNOPQRSTUVWXYZ abcdefghijklmnopqrstuvwxyz

14 point
ABCDEFGHIJKLMNOPQRSTUVWXYZ abcdefghijklmnop

18 point
ABCDEFGHIJKLMNOPQRSTUVWXYZ
abcdefghijklmnopqrstuvwxyz 1234567890

24 point
ABCDEFGHIJKLMNOPQRSTUVWXYZ
abcdefghijklmnopqrstuvwxyz 12345

30 point
ABCDEFGHIJKLMNOPQRSTU
abcdefghijklmnopqrstuvwx

36 point
ABCDEFGHIJKLMNOPQ
abcdefghijklmnopqrstu

Chart of Sans Serif type

Serif typefaces are those with embellishments or adornments on the various letters. Sans serif typefaces are those without such adornments. (See examples.)

It is a good idea to select a basic serif and a basic sans serif typeface for your body copy, and perhaps three or four basic typefaces for headlines. Generally, the pros will keep a sans serif headline type with sans serif body type and serif headline type with serif body type, but again, we remind you that this is just a guideline and not a hard-and-fast rule.

We hesitate to advise you on which typefaces to select for your magazine. Your typesetter will be able to help you with that chore. However, we would like to point out some things to keep in mind:

1. The trend among modern magazines is to go with sans serif typefaces, and the most popular of these are Helvetica (also called Helios) and Futura.

2. Another trend is away from eight- and nine-point body type in favor of 10-point type on an 11-point or 12-point slug. Newspapers used to use small type so they could squeeze in as much news and advertising as possible on a given number of pages.

Smart layout editors have come to the realization that magazines need not follow this axiom. Using larger body type results in a cleaner and classier look, not to mention easier readability. Instead of cramming everything into a given space, you have the option of adding pages or holding the size of stories and photos down to fit the space available.

Points to ponder

The format you choose and the typefaces and type sizes you select are the building blocks upon which your magazine's own unique look will rest. But there are innumerable other things which will also play a part in the final appearance of your magazine. What we consider some of the most important of these come under the headings of use of photos and trends in typography.

32   How to start your own magazine

Mezzotint

Use of photos

It is debatable whether or not a picture is worth a thousand words, but one thing is certain: proper use of good photos will help your magazine, and poor photos and improper use will detract from the image you want to convey.

A trend among better layout editors is to use fewer photos but to blow up much larger those which they do use. Photos which literally dominate a page are no longer a rarity. If you have a dynamic photo, don't be afraid to use it freely.

Cropping has always been recognized as an important function by layout editors. Seldom will you see in a magazine the complete photo just as shot by the photographer. All extraneous or unnecessary portions are cut, or cropped.

Tall, narrow photos and squat, wide photos are now used for graphic effect, with traditional "two for one" photos (twice as tall as wide) no longer the standard shape.

Layout and content 33

Line Shot

High-contrast

The half-column head-and-shoulders photo is being phased out in favor of full-column and even two-column photos. And the traditional name line is being replaced by a quotation from the story, plus identification of the person who said it.

Another recent trend among photo and layout editors is the increased use of special-effects photos, such as mezzotints, line shots, and high-contrast photos.

Trends in typography

Often the reading public is not aware of subtle changes in typography, but all you have to do is dig out an old magazine or newspaper from the attic and you will immediately be conscious of how different the publications of today look from their predecessors of just 20 or 30 years ago.

In addition to the swing to larger type and sans serif faces, mentioned earlier, here are some other trends:

• More stories and columns are being set "flush left and ragged right" instead of in standard justified columns. The result is more white space and a more casual appearance. In fact, some magazines, such as *People,* use the flush left, ragged right look exclusively. Again, it is becoming popular because editors are no longer under constraints to use every available inch of paper, as was the case of years past.

• Headlines no longer must be at the top of a story. Floating headlines, either to the left, in the center of copy, or even on a page by themselves or with a photo, are becoming popular. So are lengthy headlines, which may include 50 or 60 words and actually take the place of a lead paragraph.

• At one time, a cardinal rule of layout was that every photo needed a caption (also called cutline, because a photo is called a "cut") and every caption had to be under the photo. Not only that, captions at one time had to be mini-stories, telling about the photo in great detail. Today, captions are often much shorter, often just a brief identification of a place, and often not in sentence form. Sometimes captions are omitted completely from one or more photos in a layout when it is obvious to the readers what the photo is saying. And captions now appear on

top of photos as well as to the left and right, as well as under them.
- The copy block is another new device which is used with a photo layout. It is a cross between a caption and a story—it will not stand by itself without accompanying photos, and a single copy block will take the place of several or many captions.

One way most magazines set a copy block apart from regular body type is by setting it in a slightly larger size, such as 12 point as opposed to 10 point, and by setting it in an odd width, perhaps 18 picas instead of the regular column width, which is probably 14 picas.
- Column widths have grown in recent years from an average of 11 picas (slightly under two inches) to 14 picas (roughly 2⅜ inches). The reason is simply that three columns of 14-pica type, with 1 or 1½ picas of space between columns, will fit perfectly across a standard magazine page and four 14-pica columns will fit perfectly across a standard tabloid page.

Column widths have grown in recent years from an average of 11 picas (slightly under two inches) to 14 picas (roughly 2⅜ inches). The reason is simply that three columns of 14-pica type, with 1 or 1½ picas of space between columns, will fit perfectly across a standard magazine page and four 14-pica columns will fit perfectly across a standard tabloid page.

Column widths have grown in recent years from an average of 11 picas (slightly under two inches) to 14 picas (roughly 2⅜ inches). The reason is simply that three columns of 14-pica type, with 1 or 1½ picas of space between columns, will fit perfectly across a standard magazine page and four 14-pica columns will fit perfectly across a standard tabloid page.

Here is a paragraph set in the same type size (11 point) and the same face (times roman) as the text, at an 11-pica column width (left) and 14-pica column width (right). (*How to Start Your Own Magazine* is 26-pica column width.)

How to start your own magazine

The 14-pica column, when used with standard magazine and standard tabloid formats, enables the layout editor to "wrap" type around one side of standard ads smaller than a full page, both in magazine and tabloid formats.

4

Production

Magazine production process actually begins with the assignment of stories and sale of ads, but this chapter will be limited to the following chain or sequence of jobs in the production process:

1. Dummying out pages
2. Copy editing/typesetting
3. Pasteup
4. Making page negatives and plates
5. Going to press

Dummying out pages

The word "dummy" refers to a sheet of paper on which a variety of directions are written and drawn to show the person who pastes up the page how the layout editor wants it to look in final form. The dummy can be compared to a blueprint which carpenters follow to build a house, a road map which guides a driver, or a schematic drawing which shows an electrician where to place outlets and lines.

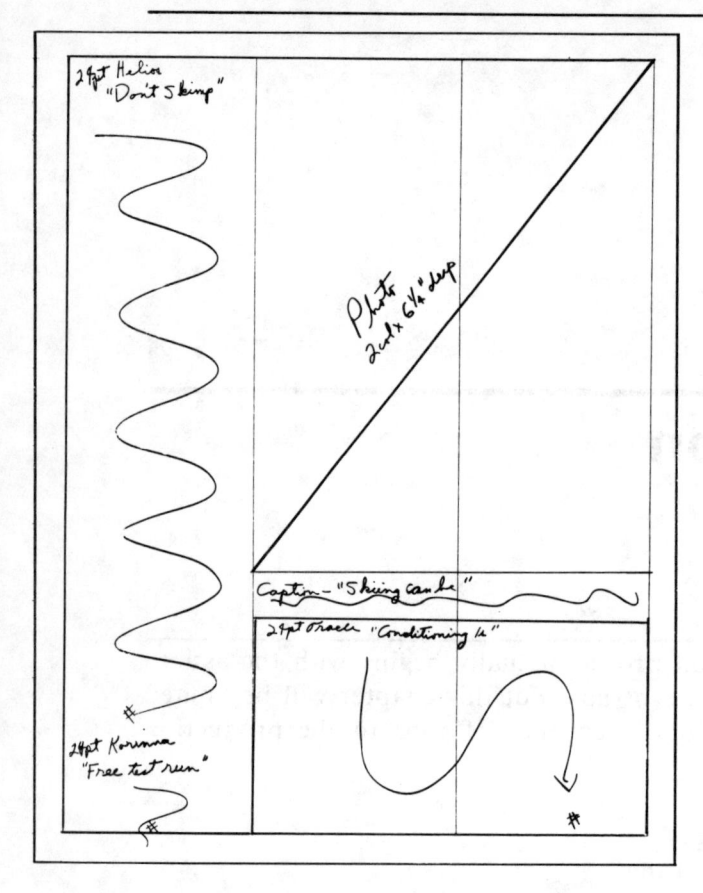

Page dummy

The dummy is sometimes the size of the actual printed page, but more often it is scaled down to 50 percent or less of actual size. It is usually marked off by inch scales running up and down both sides of the page, and by column lines.

Once you determine the specific size of the "live matter" for your pages, you can purchase your dummies from any one of a number of publishers' supply houses. Most magazines have three columns of 14 picas each, with a pica of space between columns, and half an inch of white space (border) on sides, top, and bottom. The "live matter" space usually is 7½ inches wide by 10 inches deep. Many publications prepare their own dummy sheets

Production   39

Don't Skimp When it Comes to Equipment

There has been a dramatic decline in the skier injury rate in the last 15 years. Equipment improvements have been responsible for much of the decrease.

It is of the utmost importance that you use safe equipment designed specifically for a skier of your ability. If you're in doubt about what kind of equipment to use, ask for and follow the advice of ski professionals.

The importance of safe bindings, properly installed and adjusted, cannot be stressed enough. Learn how your bindings work. Really understand them — you may be in a spot someday where you are the only one who can do something.

Care for your bindings. Lubricate them with silicone grease or spray as indicated. Friction is the culprit in many binding failures and lubrication can help; and, install mechanical antifriction devices. *Insist* they be installed on all your skis.

Don't try to economize on bindings — choose them for safety, not cost. There is no more important part of your equipment.

Don't mix binding components — they may be incompatible. A toe from one binding and a heel from another can be like having radial tires on front and regular tires on the rear. Further, don't attempt to adjust or install bindings yourself unless you really know what you're doing.

Another suggestion is to cover your bindings when you carry your skis on your car rack.

Free "Test Run"

When in doubt about skiing conditions, try them out. A number of eastern ski areas allow skiers to do just that: make a test run or two before investing in a lift ticket.

Skiing can be a safe, enjoyable, refreshing experience when a few common-sense rules of the slope are observed.   *Photographed at Bromley, Vermont*

Conditioning is Important

Pre-season conditioning is perhaps one of the more significant aspects of skiing, not only from a performance standpoint, but as a consideration in safety.

Many people who are not in condition ski, and many do so year after year safely and enjoyably. But they remember a cardinal rule: when you feel tired, or your legs are not responding well, or your coordination seems slower than normal, QUIT!

However, if the sport is to be meaningful, and, particularly, if skiing is part of a planned and "looked-foward-to" vacation, then what better way to arrive at the area than in peak condition for your age — particularly since your "out of condition" body will invariably shorten your skiing day, if you observe the proven rule of not skiing when tired.

A physical conditioning handbook is available to both downhill and cross country skiers. For your free copy, send a stamped self-addressed envelope to: Eastern Ski Association, P.O. Box 727, Brattleboro, Vermont

13

Finished page

in-house, but often it's either because they are using a bastard-size page, or because they are a large daily paper and they can save money by printing their own dummy sheets.

Dummies can be marked up in a wide variety of ways, but as long as you adopt a method and stick to it, you will eliminate possible confusion or misinterpretation on the part of the pasteup person. If you use an outside typesetting house or printer to do your pasteup, ask them to show you how they would like the dummies prepared. If you handle your own page pasteup in-house, and you haven't had experience dummying pages, either hire someone who has, or call one of your local newspapers and ask if someone on the copy desk would like to make a few bucks showing you how it's done.

In any case, remember that the trick to preparing good page dummies is to include all necessary information for the pasteup person, while avoiding the addition of anything which could be considered extraneous.

A good dummy should include:

- Page number in the appropriate place (bottom right, bottom center, top right, or wherever else you choose).
- Headline designation and "slug" for each story on the page. For example, a typical "head" designation might be "2-36 Bod. ital, 1 li," which means a two-column headline, composed of 36-point Bodoni italic type, and one line long. Following the head designation is the "slug." The slug in this sense means simply the first few words of a headline, and it serves to help the pasteup person locate the appropriate headline among those set for this issue.
- Photos are indicated by a slash or by two lines, each running from one opposite corner of the photo to the other and forming an X. Photos are usually identified by a number, which must also be on the back of the original photo.
- Captions for photos should be indicated on dummies with slugs just like those used for headlines.
- Squiggly or wavy lines are used to indicate where the type for various stories should be positioned.
- Other essential instructions for the page dummy include "jump line" designations for stories which continue on another page, and for stories which are continued from another page; slugs to indicate editor's notes, special inserts, and outquotes; and various column and cutoff rules, stars, and other special-effects type.

Can you get by without using dummies? Not if you care about the way your final product looks.

The page dummy does a lot more than simply serve as a blueprint for the pasteup person. It gives the layout editor a graphic idea of how the final page will look. It can be checked against the story list (or budget) to make sure all "must" stories and photos have been dummied. Likewise, it should always be used for a final check to make sure that all ads are dummied in and that all ads are in the right place.

Even if yours is a one-man operation, and you will be pasting all the pages up yourself, the dummy is essential. You may think you have the layout in your head, but believe us, in the crunch of deadlines, you are bound to make several mistakes without page dummies.

Copy editing

Copy editing refers to more than the editing of stories, even though the term "copy" as such refers to the typed sheets turned in by your reporters and free-lance writers.

A copy editor's responsibilities include editing copy, scaling photos to fit the size indicated on the page dummy by the layout editor, writing headlines (also designated by the layout editor), and occasionally writing photo captions, editor's notes, and other such blurbs.

On many magazines, the copy editors also dummy out pages, although it is usually the best policy to make this important function the job of a single individual. As for dummying ads, the best way to handle this is to make ad dummying the responsibility of someone in the ad department since he or she will be in daily contact with ad sales people. Ads should always be dummied in first, with the editorial material then placed in the "news hole," or remaining space. Of course, if the editor wants X number of "open pages," or pages without any ads on them, he should advise the ad department before ads are dummied in.

"style," or method of spelling certain words and using special typographical "tricks." You can develop your own stylebook for copy editors and writers or you can adopt for your own use the stylebook of the Associated Press (AP), which is used for more publications than any other.

If you have no editorial background, don't let this business of editorial style scare you. Just drop in at your local newspaper office and ask if you can buy several copies of the current AP stylebook. Or call your nearest AP bureau office and ask to buy some copies.

The stylebook will outline hundreds of specific ways of using words. For example, your writer may have typed "The meeting will take place at 10 o'clock tomorrow night." Changed to conform to AP style, this would read: "The meeting will take place at 10 p.m. tomorrow."

Why adopt the AP, or UPI (United Press International), or *New York Times* stylebook, or develop your own stylebook? To give continuity to your editorial material, to let the reader know that you are functioning according to a set rule for grammar and spelling, and to help add to the distinct personality you want to develop for your magazine.

Pasteup

Pasteup is the term applied to placing type, screened "stats" (photostatic copies), and rubylith sheets (for photos) on full-size grid sheets or page boards. The boards or grid sheets are then photographed to produce a full-page negative. And wherever rubylith was placed, there will be "windows" in the page negative. More about this later.

The grid sheet looks very much like the page dummy, except that it is full size, it has a lot of horizontal guidelines for placing type straight (usually six lines to the inch), and all lines and other marks are printed with a special blue ink which will not reproduce when the page is photographed to produce the page negative.

Such special grid sheets, just like dummies, are available from publishers' supply houses. And should your magazine be a bastard size, you can still have grid sheets made to special order.

Page pasteup may be handled by your typesetter or printer. Or you may elect to do it in-house, in which case you will save both time and money, as well as add to your quality control and provide the greatest possible leeway in getting late ads and stories into the issue.

It should be pointed out that we are assuming that you have elected to use modern "cold type," also called "phototype,"

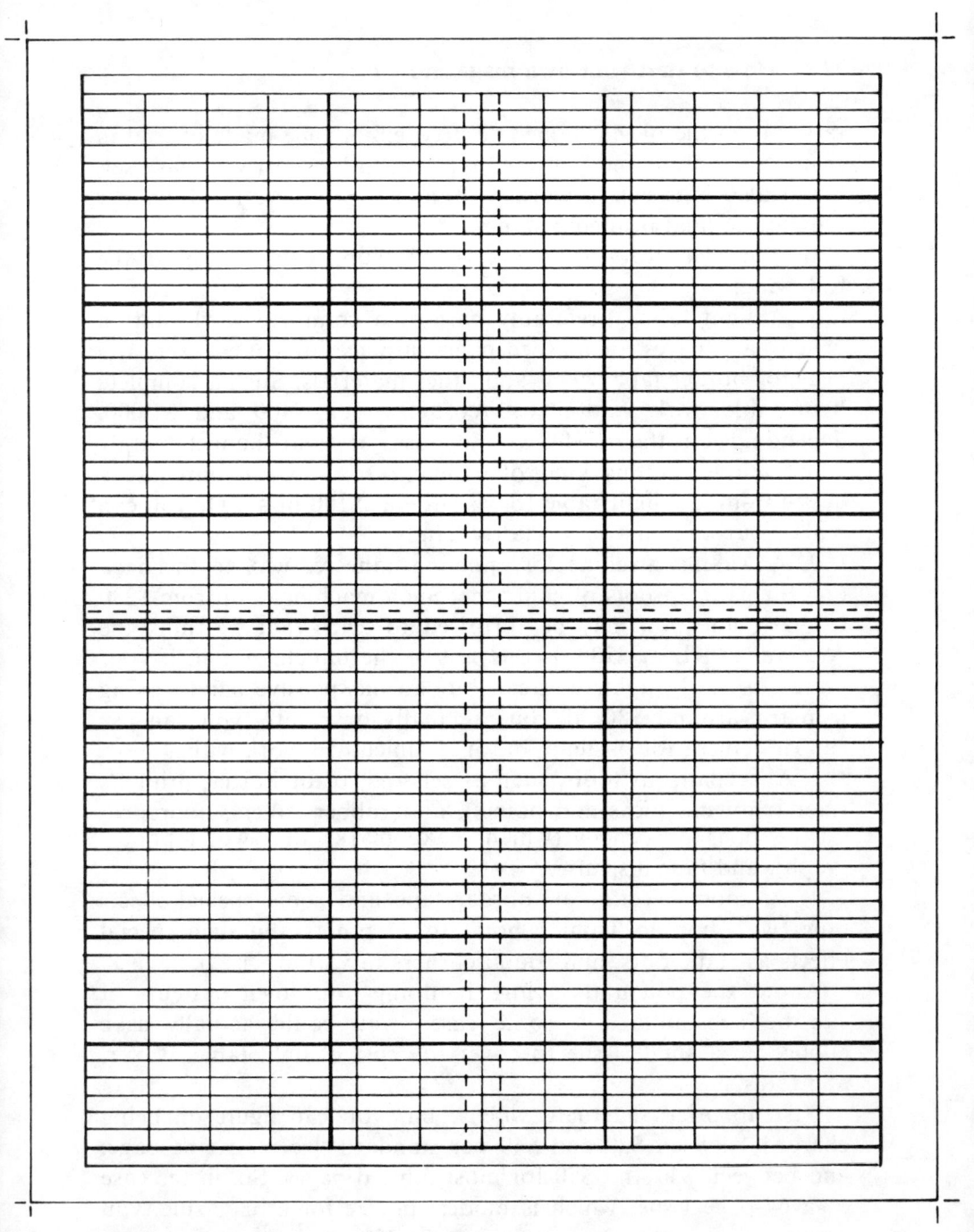

Sample grid sheet
(reduced from 7" by 10" actual size)

rather than the old-fashioned "hot type," or type made of lead in casts. Not only is modern cold type much less costly to have set, but it also is easier to work with, and it produces much crisper type in the final printed product.

If you elect to do your own pasteup, you will need the following:

1. A light table, preferably part of a complete work station which has shelves for finished pages, a place for your waxer, and pegs for border tape, ruler, and other materials. Such a complete light table/work station will cost between $400 and $1,000, depending on the model you choose. If your budget simply won't allow for this kind of expenditure, you can purchase a desk-top-model light table for as little as $100 or so. Or you can make your own, if you are fairly handy.

2. A waxing machine for applying adhesive wax to the back of your galley proofs of cold type. Such machines run from $230 to $600, and you may be surprised to learn that we think the Art Waxer III, at $230, is the best of the bunch. Again, if your budget is really tight, you can buy an inexpensive hand-waxing iron for around $30. If you are really desperate, you can use rubber cement for pasteup, but it is difficult to work with.

3. Miscellaneous tools, such as scissors, razor knives, printer's ruler (showing picas and points), and rubber rollers, nonreproducing pens or pencils (which make marks that won't photograph), and tape dispenser.

4. A good selection of border tape and some special-effects tape (with borders from 1 point to 12 points and such special effects as stars, dots, and round corners in various sizes).

About the potential savings in doing your own pasteup—it can be substantial. In some cases, you could actually save enough in a single issue to cover the cost of light table, waxer, and tools.

Pasteup prices fluctuate widely, but you can figure on being charged between $20 and $40 per standard-size magazine page, and between $30 and $50 for most tabloid pages. So, in the case of a 64-page issue, which is modest in size for a magazine, you could realize a minimum savings of $1,200.

And since we're discussing money, there's no time like the

present to talk about the operation that offers the greatest potential savings of all in the magazine production process—typesetting.

Typesetting

We mentioned previously that the way to go with typesetting is cold type, or phototypesetting, because it costs less, enables you to do your own page composition, and delivers better-quality reproduction than old-fashioned hot type.

Now, if you want to realize maximum savings on typesetting, plus achieve maximum flexibility with your production schedule

A modern phototypesetting machine, such as this Compugraphic, is not much more difficult to operate than a typewriter, and can produce dramatic savings in production costs.

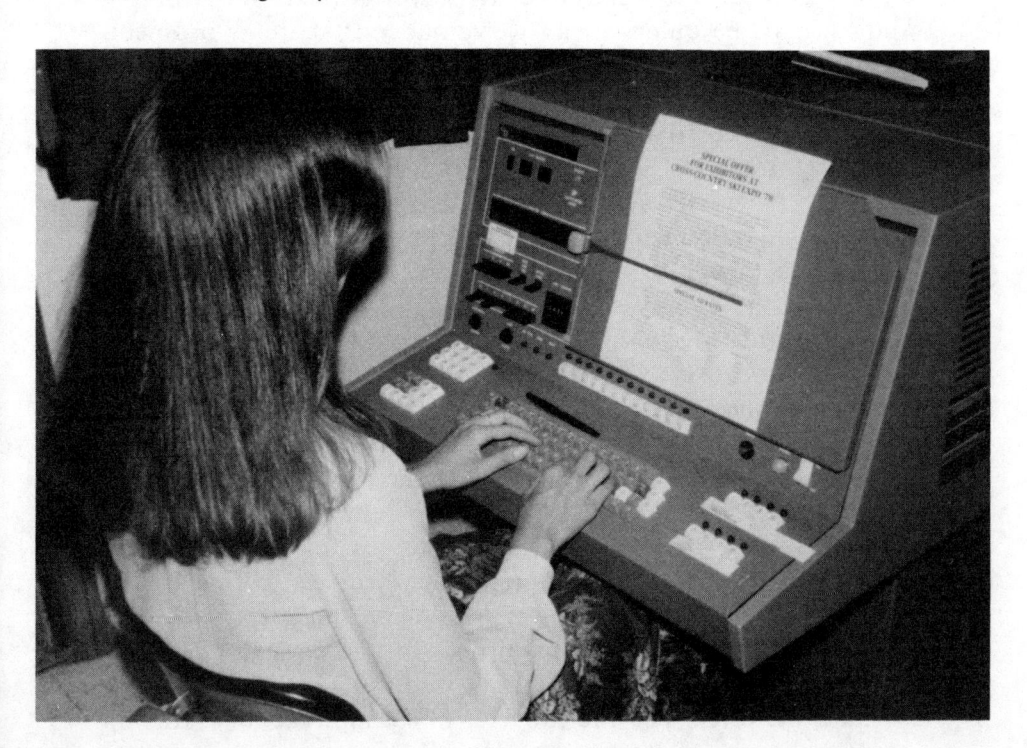

AND the look of your magazine, the way to go is to do your own typesetting.

Today's phototypesetting equipment is relatively easy to learn to operate; it takes up little office space (about as much as a small desk, in most cases); it is quite reliable (when repairs are necessary, they can usually be made by the replacement of a fuse or circuit board); and, best of all, it is relatively inexpensive to purchase or lease.

Although a dozen or so companies produce phototypesetting equipment, in our opinion the top two are Mergenthaler and Compugraphic, with Compugraphic being the undisputed leader in the field. Because of its position, Compugraphic is able to provide the most equipment for the price. Its equipment holds its resale value better than the others, too. And, since it has a high volume of business, it is able to offer an incredible variety of type styles.

Lest this begin to read like an advertisement for Compugraphic, let us be quick to say we've had our share of problems with Compugraphic equipment, including a leaky processor, bad film strip and width card, and a set of rotating lenses which has hung up on more than one occasion. But on balance, we still have to recommend Compugraphic, especially if you are located in an area where its service people are more readily accessible than those of another top company in the field.

Now we get back to the subject of potential savings. You can assume that the cost of setting type for a typical magazine page will be the same as, or slightly more than, the cost of pasting the page up. If we use a figure of $20 per magazine page on the average, we once again can realize a savings of at least $1,200 for a single issue of 64 pages. The cost of processing chemicals and photographic paper for such an issue would be somewhere in the area of $50, or even less.

Of course, we are not figuring in the cost of the typesetting machine. In the case of Compugraphic, you can purchase the Compuwriter IV model, complete with eight film strips with four different typefaces on each, plus processor and enough chemicals and photo paper to last at least six months, for about $13,000. This machine offers you the capacity of setting type in widths up to eight inches, and in 12 sizes ranging either from 6 point to 36 point, or from 6 point to 72 point.

For around $20,000 you can purchase the top of the line, Compugraphic's EditWriter 7500. It does everything that the Compuwriter IV does with one major addition. It has its own floppy disk memory system, which enables you to call a story or ad up onto the viewing screen and immediately make changes, deletions, additions, and even alterations in type size and style without manually resetting the copy.

Suppose, for example, you set a feature story in 10-point Helios (Helvetica) and you discover that it comes up short for the space allotted. Simply call the story up, change the size to 11-point or 12-point type, and instruct the machine to print it; within minutes you have a completely reset story.

In the case of ads, you can make changes easily after the advertiser sees a proof. And if you need additional copies, the EditWriter 7500 can produce as many as required.

So, assuming a savings of $1,200 per issue (which is of necessity an arbitrary figure), you could completely pay for a CompuWriter IV in 12 issues, and an EditWriter 7500 in 17 or 18 issues (excluding your other costs). And the larger your issues, the shorter the time required to pay for the machine.

The big problem for you as a new publisher is that you may not be in a position to purchase a phototypesetting machine right away. If this is the case, you may want to consider leasing or renting equipment from the manufacturer. A quick evaluation of your typesetting costs versus rental or lease cost will tell you if this alternative is a viable one. Frankly, we advise that you go with a lease or lease with purchase option as soon as you start publishing. Every month you wait will be money down the drain.

While you are calculating which way to go with typesetting, here's another bone to chew on:

If you are publishing a single magazine, and issues are monthly or quarterly, chances are you will soon discover that your sophisticated typesetting equipment is sitting idle a good deal of the time. If you hire and train a person whose exclusive responsibility will be the operation of your typesetter, you can then start accepting outside job work during your own downtime.

Some publishers find that job work is just not compatible with the requirements of producing each issue of their own publication. But some others have found that they are able to handle both in-house work and outside job work, and as a result they often make enough to pay the cost of lease payments plus the salary of the operator. We don't guarantee that you can make that much money, but it is definitely worth considering.

From pasted-up page to page negative

While we are in favor of magazine publishers' taking typesetting and pasteup operations in-house, we don't recommend this course for the remaining steps in the production process because it requires a wide variety of expensive equipment PLUS a good deal of expertise. It's better if you shop around and find a good, dependable outside company or shop to handle making page negatives, stripping up pages, making plates, and actually printing the magazine.

At this point, you must weigh quality against cost. In many cases, the best printing houses also charge an arm and a leg. On the other hand, with some careful checking, you can often find a high-quality printer whose prices are quite low.

There are ways to cut costs in the final stages of production, but they always involve a decrease in quality. For example, better-quality magazines usually reproduce photos by means of halftone negatives, which are stripped into the "windows" in page negatives before plates are made. This process is costly because of the time required to carefully strip each halftone into the page negative.

If we use a ball-park figure of $5 per halftone negative, plus a full day (eight working hours) of a printer's time to strip up a 64-page magazine, we find that the cost of reproducing photos for a single issue could easily run as much as $600 or more, and this takes into account only black-and-white photos, not full-color pictures.

By using screened stats (also called PMTs and other brand

names), you can eliminate the stripping process, since the screened stat is a positive picture which is pasted directly onto the page with the type. A second saving is realized, since the cost involved in the process of making a PMT is roughly half that of making a halftone negative. In other words, you can realize a saving of up to 50 percent, not to mention the saving in time in getting each issue out, by using PMTs instead of halftones.

The decrease in quality is least pronounced if your magazine is printed on high-quality, coated stock, and most pronounced if you use newsprint or standard offset stock. But a good lithographer can deliver PMTs which are only minimally lower in overall quality than halftones, so the choice is yours. Why not experiment, using some PMTs and some halftones in an early issue? Then compare and make your decision based on the potential savings versus possible losses of ad and subscription revenue.

Once your page negatives are finished, with or without halftones, the next step is the making of plates for the press. The only possible way of saving money here is to go with less than top-quality plate material. You can get away with it if you have a short press run, say 5,000 or 10,000 copies. But cheap plates wear out rapidly and the quality or reproduction drops as well.

The difference in cost between inferior and good-quality plates is minimal, so we recommend you go with better-quality plates and avoid the possibility of printing several thousand second-rate copies of your magazine.

Going to press

To say that you don't know anything about production is to say that you don't mind losing money.

Production is a highly technical area that takes years of comparative learning; so most publishers just starting out in the business will have to rely on the judgment of others. Those publishers who have a limited knowledge of this technical part of layout will have an edge over the rest. Just because a person is a top editorial man and has dealt with layout for years, it doesn't mean that he knows production. And advertising men who handle ads every day of their working life are usually more adept at selling them than laying them out. Production is the behind-the-scenes link with printing. And it's here that the real money can either be saved or lost.

Saving money doesn't necessarily mean sacrificing quality of the magazine reproduction either. It can actually give you a sharper finished product because a good production person is your link with the printers and their highly technical language. If the printer can't understand what you want, then it doesn't get printed.

Not only can a sharp production person help you understand what can and cannot be done on the printing press, how to work with four-color, and how to make attractive layouts for the format that you've chosen, but he also will know money-saving shortcuts that still give you high quality.

The first-time publisher will have no better friend than the printing "rep" (the intermediary between you and your printer). He should understand both printing and layout and will know what looks best. He has to—if you give him pages and they don't come out looking good, then you aren't satisfied and will tend to blame the printer rather than admit that your own judgment was poor in the first place.

After you've selected a printer, have him walk you through the entire process at the plant so you know what exactly is going to happen on printing day. This way you will be able to anticipate the coming event, and it will take away some of your anxiety. And don't be afraid to admit your ignorance. This is one person who is not going to laugh at your lack of expertise or your most ridiculous questions.

Having the rep walk you through the printing plant and the entire printing process is a must even though you might have your own production manager or art director. And they should go on the tour, too. The more knowledge you can acquire, the better. When problems arise and pressmen don't want to make the final decision, you'll be the one to get the phone call in the middle of the night. You'll be the one who has to wake up out of a sound sleep (after being up for two days straight trying to meet deadlines) and have to make instantaneous decisions. Grogginess compounded with lack of knowledge can only cost you dollars.

There are some other aspects to talk over with your production manager and printing rep when you are preparing production schedules:

• Order enough to avoid a rerun. If you think you will need 20,000 copies, run 22,000. The extra 2,000 costs very little when printed in the same press run. But to go back and remake plates and set up the presses can be very expensive. The makeready costs on a press are the same to do 20,000 impressions as to do 20. So make certain that you've ordered enough.

• Choose the right paper for the job. And, just as important, choose the right size paper. Deciding on the right paper is a critical decision which will be based on what you need from your magazine—exact reproduction, reduced weight for mailing, and type of presses used. If the wrong paper is chosen it can nullify all the other corners you have cut and costs that have been saved. You don't want to buy a fine-quality sheet for a grocery list.

Nowadays there is a paper with the right grade, weight, size, and finish for just about every conceivable printing job. Once you've decided on the finish, grade of paper, and weight, you'll need to decide on the size. If you want to do an oddball publication which is larger than usual, you're going to pay for it. Adding only one inch to the size of your publication can cost you additional hundreds of dollars that could well be spent elsewhere.

Over the course of a year, the total cost of paper can represent more than half of the total cost of publishing. So, choose your paper with the utmost care and careful planning. Only you know what you really need from your magazine. If you can afford it, go for the best; but there are other ways to have a slick-looking publication without paying for it by choosing the right paper stock.

• Many publications are designed to have two press runs—the inside body on lighter paper stock, and the outside cover, which is heavier to protect the inside pages. With two separate press runs, the cover can be run in color and the inside pages can go with either a one- or two-color plan.

• If you are trying to cut costs, it will be much more economical to plan to have only one press run. This means that you can have only one type of stock, but it will save you a great deal. You can still have color throughout the inside of the book.

• Another point to watch for when planning center folds and spreads is that the lineup of material to cross the gutter comes out exact. In order to save time for the pressmen, make certain that your art director has a dummy from the printer showing press layouts and folding diagrams. Nothing looks more unprofessional than spreads that don't match. It also costs you money when a mistake occurs. Overtime charges on this type of work, rush jobs, author's alterations, and killed matter can be incredibly costly.

• The decision of how much editorial matter each issue should carry should be related to the number of pages of advertising. There always seems to be too much to fit into each issue and the question is just how much you should squeeze in without adding greatly to production costs.

Editors always want more space than they have. The best way to determine control is by a scale which the editor must follow—59 pages of advertising will mean 53 pages of editorial matter; 60 pages of advertising will mean 52 pages of editorial; and so on, just so you always come out with an even number for a total.

To save money, make sure that the finished product you are giving to the printer has been gone over and double-checked. Are the halftones of such poor quality that they must be reshot? Is all material clearly marked with proper size and cropping instructions and color specs supplied? Are photographs and slides labeled with the numbers of the pages on which they are to appear? Is everything in sequence?

5
Printing your magazine

The hypnotic hum of a press at 4 a.m. is the most satisfying sound a publisher will ever experience. To know that all the hours of anxiety and cramming in last-minute ads are over, and the finished product—your magazine—is finally coming to life, is a rewarding experience.

The product of a publisher is his publication. No matter how large your circulation, how many pages of advertising you have, or how good the editorial product, a magazine is only as good as its quality of reproduction. Bad color in the ads can lose advertisers, and scrambled pages will bring calls from irate subscribers. If the four-color bleed cover is printed wrong with the color register off and a white line running along the side of the book, the newsstand sales can drop drastically for that month. There are no second chances once the publication has come off the presses.

When deciding on the right printer for your magazine, it is necessary to find one that not only fits your pocketbook but also does a good job. A low cost is important, but, more than that, good quality is important because that is the basis for all of your efforts. Take into consideration cost, quality, and service. If all a printer can do is print the publication, but not give you any delivery on the finished product, you may want to look elsewhere.

Before approaching a printer to solicit bids for the printing costs, you will have to decide exactly what it is that you want the printer to do for you. Be able to tell him the exact format you have decided on (for example, tabloid; slick; and so on), how much color (four- and two-color) will be used throughout the book, how many pages you are expecting to run per issue, how many photographs per issue, and what your press run will be per issue.

After a printer understands exactly what you want, he will be able to show you ways to cut costs by standardizing your product, laying out the paper so that all color work will fit on the same form, and reducing the weight of the paper to save on mailing costs and type of press that is best suited to your publication.

There is not just one standard answer to what type of printing process should be used: offset, letterpress, or gravure. The technical requirements of your own magazine will be the deciding factor for choosing a printing process. Briefly, here are the differences between the various printing methods:

- Offset lithography uses the planographic method in which the ink is transferred from the plate to a rubber blanket and then onto the paper. This is a relatively slow press run because of the chemical nature of the offset process and should be considered only for runs of up to 750,000. The plate charges are the cheapest, compared to the other two printing methods. A disadvantage to the offset method is that it cannot print on the lightest-weight papers and it wastes more paper during a press run.

- Letterpress printing is done from a raised metal relief plate called an electrotype. The ink image is transferred directly onto the paper in this process. Since letterpress is done from metal plates, the makeready time is high, but chrome-coated plates can accommodate press runs into the millions.

- Gravure uses a depressed surface for the image. The image is etched into a copper cylinder which rotates in a mat ink. The excess ink is wiped off the cylinder by a steel blade, and the remaining ink in the etched-out copper is transferred onto paper. While the gravure platemaking cost is high, once the cylinder is placed on the press the makeready process is simple and the time is fast. Only if your publication is going to be able to fill up a 48-page gravure press and have runs of over 800,000 should you consider this method for printing.

There is no set answer to which process is best for your magazine. It will depend on the specifications of your publication and the quality you expect. Other aspects must also be taken into consideration:

- Do the printers deliver the papers to the distributing company?
- Do they have the capacity for shipping to other parts of the country?
- Are they set up for the technical aspects of mailing and ZIP Coding?
- Can they provide wrap covers or the less expensive shrink-wrap covers for mailing?

While one printer's costs might be a little higher than another's, if he offers all the services that you require then he will be the one to consider.

Some printers won't touch small jobs because of the added work needed to change the presses. Small jobs under 75,000 per run will usually be recommended to those printers that are in the business of doing small jobs, since a press run of this number usually takes only a few hours.

A close working relationship between a publisher and a printer is necessary for ultimate coordination. It will be necessary for you to familiarize yourself with printing terminology. Printers have their own way of talking; if you constantly have to stop the pressman and ask him to repeat what he said so that you can understand it, not only will you be losing valuable time when a quick decision is necessary, but you also will alienate yourself from the printers. All your objectives such as the quality of reproduction, trim, and placement of mailing labels should have been understood long before the publication is on the presses. There is no room for changing your mind once those presses start rolling; it will only cost you money for every decision that is changed.

Books are available at your local library that will familiarize you with technical printing jargon. Since you will be watching the first few press runs to see that everything goes smoothly, this subject is a must on your reading list.

For the first six issues or so, the publisher should be at the press throughout the entire process from printing to binding. This might mean over 24 hours without sleep, but it will be worth it in the end. While printers like to work without interference, they don't seem to mind the publisher's being there; some prefer it rather than having to make decisions on their own without your consent. It is at this point that tact is vital. A printer's shop is his domain, and you are the intruder there.

Be polite, but don't be afraid to speak up if you feel something is going wrong. And at no cost should you get into an argument with the printer. Not only will this isolate you from the problem, but thousands of copies could go through the press before the disagreement is cleared up. This is the time for quick and precise decisions—not hesitation. If you don't know what you are doing, don't try to fake it. Tell the printer and rely on his judgment in the situation. After all, he's done this type of work for years and is a skilled craftsman.

If you do have a legitimate complaint about the work that has been run, tell the printer. But lead off the complaint with a statement of understanding of the printer's knowledge of his trade and his years of experience, and what a good working relationship the two of you have together. Then tell him that you think there is one small problem (no matter how great, state that it isn't a catastrophe and that it can be solved easily with cooperation) that should be worked out.

Explain what the problem is going to do to your business and why. If the color on one form is bad, state that you can lose advertisers, say that type bleeding through the page will bring calls from irritated subscribers. The man is a printer and not a

Printing your magazine 57

magazine publisher and can't be expected to understand all the problems of your business, too.

In taking into consideration which printer should be the one to go with, you must realize that the small magazine publisher is at a disadvantage nowadays. Over the past years, many printing plants have gone under due in part to the folding of many newspapers and magazines. Usually when you solicit a bid for costs, the printer will have the upper hand and may even designate what weights of paper you may select from, when the magazine can fit into his printing schedule, and what is the availability of combination forms for late closings.

The best thing a publisher of a small-circulation magazine can do is to form a cooperative working relationship with the printer. In this day and age of recurring paper crises, it is necessary to find out what a printer's availability of paper is. If a printer can't guarantee paper, there is no need to talk any further.

Many times printers will join paper pools and buy large quantities along with other smaller printers. This way they are assured of a year's supply. If you have established yourself as a steady and reliable customer, you won't have to worry about being the first man out if a paper crunch hits.

Understand, too, that in every cost quotation, there is a clause which states that the publisher will pay any rising costs of paper or other expenses that may be incurred by the printer. Prices can rise from 6 percent to as much as 30 percent in a year, so be prepared.

The most important thing is to understand the terms of the contract before you sign it. Consider everything that is included in the contract and everything that is not. Printers do have a way of quoting a price and then when the final bill arrives, asking a price much higher than what you expected—due to the cost of preparing the color work, plate charges, or anything else that might not have been added to the initial tally. It will be up to you to see that everything has been included and to find out how much the other costs will be.

Terms of payment have also become something of a problem for the smaller magazine publisher. Many printers want payment in advance until credit has been established. They are the ones dictating policy, and there seems to be no way around this. So, for the new magazine publisher not sure of an immediate return, this means a secure capital base from which to draw.

As much as printers are leery of magazines that come and go and are never heard of again, the new magazine publisher still has a right to know about the solidity of the printer he is considering. All the guarantees of quality and dependability are nothing if the printer goes under. Be sure that you find an established firm to work with so that you aren't caught at deadline with all your negatives ready and nowhere to take them.

Once you've found a printer, do the best to stick with him and work out any problems that occur. Not only is switching printers time-consuming, but it also can cause a lowering of standards with your product.

6
Holding costs down

No one facet of publishing a magazine can be segregated from the others and labeled "most important" or "least important." Each function—editorial, advertising, circulation, promotion, production, and printing—is like a piece of a puzzle, a part of a mosaic. Each is necessary and vital to the total product. Failure in any one facet can very definitely result in the failure of your magazine.

Promotion, advertising sales, and circulation all directly contribute to revenues, while editorial, production, and printing are often seen simply as expensive necessities. In fact, feuding between editorial and advertising staffers is practically a tradition on publications of all types.

What some ad people fail to realize is that without a vital, dynamic editorial product, there would be no magazine. Nonetheless, one of your chief functions as publisher will be to keep a constant watch on the cost of producing your magazine.

Planning the initial budget

You already know what you want your magazine to become.

In planning it, you have determined its scope of circulation, its format, and the estimated revenues from retail sales, subscriptions, and ad sales. You also know, based on your efforts at raising capital, just how much you have to work with until revenues match and surpass expenses.

The trick now is to develop budgets for every department of your magazine which will enable you to survive the start-up period without being forced to scramble for additional capital. The best way to accomplish this is to calculate exactly how little you can budget for each publishing function and still get the job done. Don't just take the amount of available capital and then parcel out various percentages of it for each department, or you'll run dry in short order.

And don't expect your staffers (if your magazine is large enough in scope to have staffers other than yourself) to squeeze every dollar for all it's worth—as employees, they simply can't be expected to view your magazine project as a life-or-death proposition. If it folds, they will simply go on to another job. You, on the other hand, will have the creditors to satisfy.

Let's suppose that you have borrowed $100,000 from your local bank, and you are starting your magazine as a proprietorship. The publication will be one of the new breed of "city magazines," and for the sake of argument, let's say that it is called *Madison,* since it will serve the residents of Madison, Wisconsin.

You decide that the first issue will be 48 pages, based on estimates of initial ad support at 24 pages (a 50-50 ratio of ads to editorial matter is an excellent one, especially for a brand-new magazine).

Your page rate is $1,000 for a black-and-white ad, and so you anticipate revenues of $24,000 for this issue. Of course, in arriving at that figure you forgot to take into account that all ads placed through agencies will be entitled to a 15-percent agency commission (standard for the industry). You also forgot that you are offering charter advertisers a flat 15-percent discount off the top. So your ad sales for this issue will actually be more like $17,000.

Now, even if you are very aggressive in your collection

activities, chances are that between 5 percent and 10 percent of the total ad billing for this issue will be uncollectible. Ad agencies sometimes go out of business. Others will simply be deadbeats. Occasionally, there will be a disagreement about payment for an ad because it wasn't placed according to instructions (for example, right-hand page, far forward) or because the advertiser was unhappy with the quality of reproduction. (In such cases, the best rule is always to settle the disagreement in favor of the advertiser. You may lose this particular sale, but in the long run, you will be way ahead. Demanding payment for a disputed ad may result in payment but you will most likely lose the advertiser AND the agency, which might have been in a position to place ads for some of its other clients as well.)

One way to minimize loss of ad revenue in case of disputed ads is to suggest to the agency that you will provide a "make-good" ad. Granted, the second insertion will not bring in any revenue, but at least you will collect on the first insertion. Another way of looking at it is that by giving a make-good ad, you collect 50 percent of the rate card price for each insertion, rather than 0 percent for a single insertion. AND you have avoided creating further hard feelings on the part of the advertiser.

In any case, your $17,000 in revenue for the first issue will be cut to $15,000 or $16,000 because of the factors we just described. There is one final fly in the ointment—don't assume that you will collect 100 percent of the invoices right away. Most magazines find that about 50 percent of the advertisers pay within 30 days. Another 25 percent pay during the second 30 days. And the remainder may come trickling in for as long as six months or more.

It is a good rule of thumb that after 60 days, your chances of collecting are cut in half with each succeeding 30-day period which goes by. For this reason, the best policy on collections must be a tough one. Many young magazines go under because of failure to collect on accounts receivable.

Ad agencies and independent advertisers often maintain a "wait-and-see" attitude toward payment to new magazines. They figure that if you make it, they can always pay later, and if you do go under, they got *x* number of free ads by delaying payment.

There is only one way to deal with this kind of thinking. Make sure you and your ad salesmen include the subject of payments in all ad presentations. Explain that you are aware of the widespread practice of delaying payments to new magazines, but you don't intend to allow advertisers to pursue this practice.

State that you are producing a first-rate publication and providing ad space at a fair price. In return, you expect to be paid promptly—in other words, within the standard 30-day period. Explain that all accounts more than 30 days overdue will be turned over to your attorney for collection.

It is extremely important that you pursue this tough talk with action, or word will soon get around that *Madison* magazine is a soft touch, and at that point you are as good as dead.

If an advertiser or agency takes offense at your policy and advises you that they don't intend to advertise because of it, you really aren't out anything. Who needs deadbeat advertisers? Unless you can collect for ads, you are worse off than if you had never sold them, because you have now incurred the expense of printing the ads, and of allowing the additional space in your magazine.

The "tough collection" approach will weed out many deadbeats and save you a good deal of grief. An additional way to avoid picking up deadbeats for advertisers is to use a service such as that provided by Dun & Bradstreet to determine the credit rating of potential advertisers.

It is a mistake to assume because an advertiser is a major corporation, or because it has a well-known ad agency, that it is a good risk. Large corporations and agencies are notoriously slow payers. Sure, you'll eventually get your money; but in the meantime, inflation is eroding its value and your debtor is collecting interest or using that money of yours for his own purposes.

Of course, as a new magazine, you may decide that you are better off living with this kind of slow-pay problem and realizing less income from such advertisers rather than doing without the revenue altogether. This is where you (and possibly your accountant) must determine whether such a practice ultimately costs you more in expenses than you realize in income. If your ad rates are such that there is very little profit margin, then you most surely will lose in such cases.

One way to eliminate the slow-pay problem, other than the "tough collection" pitch during sales calls, is to require all new advertisers to pay 50 percent of the ad cost with their orders until "credit is established." This will cut your slow-pay problem in half, and will also serve as an incentive for the advertiser to pay the remainder of his bill, since he's already committed halfway.

As soon as you feel your magazine is strong enough, you should crack down on slow payers by advising them that until their account is settled, remaining ads must be paid in advance.

Maintaining a tough posture on collections is far and away the most difficult single task facing any publisher. Even well-established magazines, and experienced publishers who should know better, fall prey to letting advertisers get away with slow pay or no pay.

The firm approach to collections will not hurt you, but will help you both in hard cash coming into your account, and in helping your new magazine win the respect of the business community. Remember, every single ad agency and client you deal with is also faced with the problem of collections on accounts receivable. Your tough approach will be admired, not scorned.

Deciding where to cut expenses

So much for collections. Now let's get back to the subject at hand—budgeting for the various publishing functions.

We now know that ad revenues for the first issue of *Madison* magazine will be $15,000 to $16,000, and that at best, only $8,000 or so will come in within 30 days of the invoice date. It is also safe to say that it will take a good six months of publishing before monthly collections for ad sales equal or even approach the gross ad sales for the issue published in a given month. And, since ad sales will grow steadily for the first year or two, you will always be in a catch-up position during this period. It means that expenses will be growing with circulation and ad sales, but income will be lagging behind.

So, unless you have a healthy nest egg to fall back on until income balances with expenses, you MUST figure another way of staying in business during this period. That second way is to cut budgets, then cut some more, and then cut some more, until every bit of fat is eliminated.

The trick in doing this successfully is to cut most drastically those expenses which are not visible to the advertisers, but to limit cutting in those areas where there is high visibility.

To put it another way, you must reduce costs but not the image of a first-rate publication. Here are a few suggestions:

- Hold long-distance telephone calls to an absolute minimum. Unless you are calling to trace a late ad (which means revenue to you), write a letter instead. When you must call long distance, ALWAYS call person-to-person. Sure, it costs more, but you will have to pay only when you get the right person on the line. When you call a large agency or corporation, you seldom reach your party on the first try. He's either in a meeting, out to lunch, out of town on business, sick, or on another line. And while someone is trying to track him down in the office, you may be put on hold for a long, long time. Person-to-person calls eliminate all of this hassle, and you can still leave word for the party to call back without its costing you a cent until the call is actually returned.

- Don't send out your media kits to every possible advertiser. Send media kits only to your best prospects. For others, send a letter instead, advising that you will be happy to send a media kit if they are interested in learning more about your magazine. This approach will save you several dollars in the cost of each kit, plus perhaps a dollar or more for the postage. And it will key you in to those who do ask for a media kit, since they have obviously become better prospects.

- Don't start out with an expensive office in the downtown district of your city or town. You and your ad people will be

Holding costs down 65

doing all the calling at other offices, so you simply do not need a fancy office in the high-rent district. We know of many magazines which were started in the garage or basement of the publisher's house, and in no case was the site of their office a hindrance to their success. However, if your address is obviously in a residential neighborhood, get a post office box and use it as your official address.

You will find that even major corporations and ad agencies use post office boxes because of the volume of mail they receive, and a post office box will often convince potential advertisers that yours is a large organization.

Another advantage of using a post office box is that you can now get a first-class return-postage permit from your post office. Subscribers can send in response cards which are postage-paid, and advertisers can also send back surveys and other inquiries with a postage-paid card. This type of response card works best when you send out a mailing to announce a special issue, perhaps with discounted ad rates. The 25 cents the post office charges you is covered in the sale the card produces.

- You can save a good deal of money on phone bills if you don't let the phone company know that your phone is being used for business. Of course, this means that you can't list your business in the white or yellow pages, so you must make a determination whether the savings in phone cost is offset by the possible loss of business from people seeking to call you.

In most cases, it won't hurt, since you are making all the initial calls on potential advertisers, and since your business card, letterhead, and other materials all carry your phone number and mailing address.

- Don't make the mistake of trying to hold costs down by ordering minimum amounts of letterheads and envelopes. The general rule in printing is that the bulk of the cost is in preparation and platemaking.

We'd suggest a minimum order of 2,000 letterheads, 1,000 second sheets, and 2,000 envelopes. This amount should hold you until ad revenues catch up with expenses and you can order more.

Ordering 10,000 or 20,000 letterheads and envelopes is a

mistake because (a) you may move your office or otherwise change your mailing address before most of them have been used, (b) you may decide to change the look of your letterheads and envelopes, and (c) you'll have to store all these envelopes and letterheads; envelopes sometimes absorb moisture in the summer and you'll find that some of them have sealed themselves.

• Don't rush out and purchase all kinds of brand-new office equipment. You can save money and have much less down time with equipment if you purchase the best available used equipment. For example, buy one rebuilt IBM Executive or Selectric model office typewriter with carbon ribbon to be used for business letters. Remember that your business letters reflect your magazine. The IBM office electric models will give you the best possible results.

We have found that the best portable typewriters on the market are the various Smith-Corona electric models. In fact, we have two such typewriters which have been banged around both in the office and on business trips for many years, and both still perform admirably.

The Smith-Corona portables can be used for writing editorial and ad copy, for typing interoffice memos, and for business trips.

The advantage of both IBM and Smith-Corona is that both are leaders in the field, and you will be able to get either repaired with a minimum of fuss anywhere in the country.

Should you buy or lease a copier? We don't think so, at least at first. Simple carbon copies will work in most instances, and if you need a Xerox-type copy when sending one to an advertiser, use the coin-operated copier at the nearest post office, drugstore, or currency exchange.

• Should you employ a telephone answering service, or purchase a telephone answering machine? If someone will be in your office at all times during business hours, the obvious answer is no.

If yours is a one-man or two-man operation, and you are out a good deal of the time during office hours, by all means get some means of taking calls in your absence.

We have found that the answering machines are the less preferable of the two choices. For one thing, a lot of people simply will not talk to a machine, but will hang up instead. Then, you will find that sometimes, you forget to turn the machine on. Finally, these machines have a limited capacity for messages and also have a habit of going on the blink just at the wrong time—such as when you are away on a two-week business trip.

The answering service, on the other hand, provides a personal method of taking calls. Often, the service will answer with your company name, so that the caller isn't even aware that he is talking to a service. You can leave special instructions: "Tell callers I'll be back in an hour to return their call," or "I'm away on business but will return their call tomorrow." If you are out of town for an extended period, you can still call in to your service to get all calls. Then, if one of them requires immediate attention, you can handle it right away.

One way to hold costs of an answering service to a minimum is to take the service just for business hours. Answering services often offer a 12-hour service, or even a 24-hour service for people such as doctors, but as a publisher, you don't need these.

• Even such equipment as desks cost a lot of money. If your operation is a small one, you can "create" desks by placing a door panel across two filing cabinets. Not only do you create a large work area on top, but you also save a good deal of space by combining the cabinets and desk. And, surprisingly, this kind of desk is quite attractive-looking as well as functional.

7
Building circulation

The general slant of your magazine and its editorial content will determine your areas of circulation. Once you have decided whom you want to contact, then comes the problem of deciding the best way to reach those people as well as the most economical way.

Your magazine might appeal to various audiences such as the local community market, the regional market, the national market, or the highly vertical, specialized fields. The type of people that you are trying to reach will be the deciding factor as to what approach to take.

Building up subscriptions to make a totally paid reading audience can be time-consuming as well as costly. Many publications also go on newsstands to build circulation, but many distributors are leery of taking on new customers without a proven track record. Unless they see a particularly bright future for a publication like yours, the chances are slim of its going on newsstands right away.

In the beginning, some publications don't even attempt to have a paid circulation, but instead focus on being a free giveaway with distribution house-to-house or at localized pickup areas. Some advertising agencies look down on giveaway publications and tend to look only at magazines with ABC-verified (Audit Bureau of Circulation) audiences of paid subscribers.

There are ways of creating circulation with minimal time and money investments. These should be analyzed carefully, though, to ensure profitability before you pick the one for your specific market.

The Audit Bureau of Circulation publishes a booklet naming more than 350 subscription agencies which publishers may enlist to increase circulation. Each agency has a different way of promoting and has a specific market that it appeals to. Careful investigation should turn up the agencies that would be best for your magazine. These agencies cost comparatively little and you don't need that much upfront money, either.

If you have a highly specific audience that you want to reach, such as gun collectors, you might want to approach dealers and manufacturers and offer them a free ad in your publication in exchange for their mailing list. This way you can mail out teasers and subscription blanks to exactly the people who will be interested in your product.

Or, you can have the dealer send out a direct-mail piece about your magazine with their billings in return for a free ad in your publication.

Another overlooked area is that of associations. Many associations would like to have their own publication to send out to members, but the people who run most organizations have little publishing experience. You can step in and tell them how great your publication is and what you can do for them. They in return can include the price of your subscription as part of their membership dues. You'll have to be the one to approach most organizations; always be ready to give them what they want—within limits, that is. Start off not offering too much. When they ask for what you had intended to give them anyway, they will think that they have scored a negotiating coup.

Magazines that aren't in direct competition with each other will many times do co-op advertising for subscribers; in this way the cost of an advertisement will be borne by several publications. This practice does have a tendency not to give the results that were hoped for, though, unless your magazine is advertised in another publication with a similar readership. You can't sell ten-speed bicycles to the Kawasaki crowd.

Or you might try doing trade-out advertising with a magazine not directly related to yours. You advertise in their publication with a subscription blank and they advertise their magazine in your publication. Sporting magazines not related to each other can turn up a good response, such as a skiing publication and a tennis publication.

You may opt for a per-inquiry (PI) type of ad. This works so that when you advertise your magazine in another publication you agree to pay the publisher a small percentage for each subscription that is sold.

Always check and audit your response when applying any of these methods and check for impulse buyers who cancel their subscriptions later on. You are looking for the subscriber who is going to renew after his initial subscription has terminated. Don't waste your money by trying to get your magazine's name out in front of the public to impress people. An uninterested market won't notice what you are trying to sell unless they are ready to buy. Those are the buyers you are trying to find—not notoriety.

Advertising gift subscriptions in your own publications can be a good idea. And don't think it's only at Christmastime that you can do this, either. Continue this campaign all year long. Give subscribers a discount depending on the number of subscriptions that they sign up for.

There are endless ways of creating circulation by working deals with people. But never let others think that they are doing you a favor helping you out. Approach them with the idea that you are both promoting each other and neither one is giving a handout to the other.

Consider asking your local bank to give magazine subscriptions away for those opening new accounts; have retail stores give subscriptions away to those customers spending a certain total dollar amount in their store; give neighbors an incentive to sell subscriptions to their friends, fellow church members, and others. You can put point-of-purchase displays in stores with subscription cards that people can take and fill out later on, or you might try a type of standing display in doctors' and dentists' offices.

Remember, too, that the time of the year should be considered in reaching potential subscribers. If a city is shoveling out from a blizzard, you won't want to run television and radio commercials at this time. These people will be more interested in getting the tow truck to pull their car out of a snowbank than in sitting down and subscribing to your publication.

Hit your market at the height of its season and also just before that season begins. Many people will anticipate the coming season and start reading everything they can to be informed before it actually arrives. Do a mailing to all those doctors and nurses who might be anticipating a coming convention—even have a booth at that show to collect subscribers.

Do a deal in which you offer one issue free and if the customer isn't happy, he doesn't have to accept the rest of the magazines or pay anything; he simply sends back a card stating that you should cancel his subscription.

Whenever appealing to readers, hit them with the "big savings if you subscribe now" routine. This is sound psychology because everyone today is looking to save a dollar or two.

Always set a goal as to how many new subscribers you want to add; when you have reached this level, reassess your present standing. Go over the actual out-of-pocket expenses and see how much it has cost you per subscriber to attain your circulation level. Keep accurate facts and figures not only for your own records, but for the Internal Revenue Service as well.

The best way to keep a subscriber is to keep him happy. Your "customer service department" will most likely be anyone who happens to answer the telephone when it rings. The old saying that the customer is always right is the only policy to follow. Give the irate person on the other end of the phone the chance to tell you what the problem is and agree to whatever it is that he is saying.

Always be sure to find out exactly what is wrong and if the

problem is a recurring one. Never argue with the customer. If you are polite, usually the angry person will calm down and stop being defensive and you can win his confidence. It is at this time that you find out what it is that the customer wants you to do for him, and how you can make him happy again.

Customers cannot be expected to understand your publishing and computer problems. Assure them that you will remedy the problem and thank them for calling it to your attention. If you cannot give a specific answer right then and there, tell them you will look into the matter and notify them as soon as you have found out what went wrong.

Always follow up and let your customers know what you did for them. Let the subscribers feel that they have been taken care of by a professional whom they can depend on and respect as much as they do the publication that they read.

Competition among publications nowadays is the determining factor as to how much you should charge per issue for the magazine. If you are reaching a market that many other magazines are reaching, then you will have to keep the price per copy in line with what others are charging. But if you have a highly specific audience, you can charge top dollar for the publication.

Many times the cost of the subscription does little more than pay for the cost of mailing the magazine out. All you do is to break even with the post office and the subscriber. It's the advertising that brings home the gravy.

A highly vertical publication can charge top dollar for a magazine and not only pay for postage, but also pay for a part of the quality printing for the publication. Your product must be solid and something that readers cannot get anywhere else; then they'll be more than happy to pay for what they want.

Advertisers look not only at the total circulation figures but at the quality of those readers, too. If you are aiming for a specific market, an advertiser would be happier to pay for a guaranteed 5,000 potential buyers than to reach 50,000 people who couldn't care less about his product. So, it's not only how many readers you have but also who they are that counts.

To do demographic surveys of your readers, send out postage-guaranteed cards with a few specific questions that you would like answered. Keep the questions direct and to the point. Too many items to answer will make a person tend to throw the card away rather than take more than a few moments to answer the inquiry. By sending the surveys out with your regular billing and renewal slips, you save the added postage of a separate mailing.

The answers to these questions can be applied to your advertising sales kits along with your rate card and mechanical requirements for ad materials. Advertisers like to see exactly whom they are reaching for their dollars.

The biggest aid to circulation is reader involvement. If the reader doesn't like what he is reading, he won't want to subscribe, no matter how good an offer you make him. Editorial content is a primary selling force in the race for circulation growth.

8
Promotion is important, too

No magazine is so small or so large that it can overlook sales promotion. In the publishing field, you continually have to toot your own horn and let everyone know not only what you are doing for them, but what you are doing for the industry, community, nation, and Mother Earth. Let everyone know what your magazine does that the others don't and tell people why they should be reading it.

Larger magazines with funds appropriated for sales promotion can afford to spend lots of dollars spreading their names around, but small magazines are going to have to place their promotion dollars carefully. If done correctly, you can combine your promotions to sell advertisers and subscribers at the same time instead of having two separate campaigns, one aimed at each market.

While there is an argument that promotion will never actually sell anything, it is common knowledge that you must have it no matter what.

The way to solve a lot of problems and avoid the risk of spending unwanted dollars is to formulate a promotion objective. Decide what you want to do and where you want to do it and then attack only that area. Develop a strong, identifiable approach and then stick to it. A new magazine needs to show its continuing credibility and to develop its name into something the public identifies with automatically. This means that in the beginning you must reinforce your name and message by repetition, not by creative ways of impressing the public.

A good promotion campaign will single out your publication from all the other publications that might be of similar quality. People are usually not aware of the differences in existing publications, even though to you the differences might seem like night and day. To the average reader, it must be pointed out and reinforced that there are differences, what they are, and how your magazine is better than all the rest.

A good promotion campaign will help you show advertisers that the people you are appealing to are exactly the ones that they should be reaching for the products their clients offer. It will show advertisers why people in your market are exciting, intelligent, affluent, and on the move. If advertisers think that your publication is one of the best in the field today, of course they will want to make certain that they advertise in it.

Internally, you have to keep up the morale of your employees, too. A good promotion campaign will reinforce employees' views of the importance and dynamism of the magazine.

When planning a promotion campaign, decide on a direction and follow that direction through to the end. Don't change in midstream.

Decide on what it is that you want to accomplish. Perhaps it is trying to reach new subscribers, making your magazine appeal to a high caliber of people, reaching a specific type of advertiser, or providing local appeal. Whatever it is, decide on a strong central theme that will carry the entire campaign. A simple but hard-hitting slogan will be easy to remember and also should say everything with one statement. You might even be able to tie your editorial pages in with the theme somehow by interviewing prominent people every month or doing a survey on certain manufacturing products, for example.

When you've done this, you'll want to send out press releases to noncompetitive magazines, metropolitan newspapers, radio

Promotion is important, too 77

and television stations, organizations, and any other company or person that you feel might be able to help you spread the word about what you are doing. Make the press release something vital to the community and world, not just the old boring facts and figures that come across an editor's desk a hundred times a day. Give it some pizzazz and show how your publication is relevant to today.

Once you've decided where releases should go, determine how often you should send them out. If you send out too many, not only will you be wasting money, but people will tend to overlook what you say. If you don't send out enough, though, you're going to miss a great portion of your market.

Besides press releases, you might also want to try sending out a reprint of an article that has run in your magazine if you feel that it is especially good and fits in with your main objective. It is also a good idea to phone the people to whom you are sending releases to introduce yourself and make the communication more personal.

If you can't afford to hire an outside specialist, make certain that the person who will be handling your promotion will be coordinating all details, measuring the results of the campaign, and seeing that the original objective is still being pursued.

Another good way to promote your publication is to attend trade and consumer shows. Take a booth to sell subscriptions and be on hand to answer questions. You'll be able to meet many of the top people in your field and exchange ideas with them.

Just because you have a small budget, it doesn't mean that you can't be in there hitting just like the big boys. It just means that you have to be a little more careful of how you do it. It could also be an excellent idea to schedule one of your issues around that show. Write about the manufacturers and what they are doing. By promoting them, you are promoting yourself, too.

Be aware, though, that trade shows are not good places to sell advertising space. Retailers, manufacturers, and others are there to sell their own products, not to be sold ads by you. All you want to do at the trade and consumer shows is to make yourself known.

If you can't afford a booth, attend the show and make a point of meeting the people who are important to you. Consider hosting a cocktail party and inviting potential advertisers—but remember: no selling here, either. If you've done an article about a specific manufacturer, for example, have the manufacturer put a blowup of that article on display, reprinted compliments of your magazine. And consider taking out a small ad in the show booklets and programs.

Many times at conventions and seminars a portion of the program will be devoted to a discussion of issues by prominent people in the field. Why shouldn't you be one of those noted authorities? Give a talk on something that is of interest to everyone at the show. This approach brings you into close working contact with others in the industry, while adding to the prestige and credibility of your magazine.

A common mistake you don't want to make is to overlook the quality of your own ads that you place in your own publication or in others for gaining reader interest. Your ad is a reflection of your magazine, so make sure that it is of the same caliber as those of advertisers to whom you want to appeal.

A bad ad will do more damage than no ad at all. And keep things simple. You can say only so much in a given space. If you cram in every idea you have, chances are the reader won't pick up any of what you are trying to say.

Don't try to reach an entire market with your ad. Personalize the ad so that it appeals to the reader—the one actually reading the ad. Tell him what your publication is going to do for him, not the country. How is *he* going to benefit from it? What is it going to do for *him*?

Keeping your name out in front of the public is hard work. It's something that has to be worked at constantly and updated often. Don't think that promotion is the least of all your worries. Never underestimate the importance of a good promotion campaign. *You* know the benefits to be derived from reading your own magazine, but to other people it is just one of many they see every day. It is up to you to sell both readers and potential advertisers.

9

How to sell ad space

No matter how good your editorial product or how clever the concept and design of the magazine, without advertising dollars to keep paying those printing bills, you won't have a magazine for long. Advertising is the main component in producing your publication—without it you can't exist.

Even if you have a high subscription price, with continually rising postal costs you will be lucky if the subscription price covers labeling, handling, and mailing costs. You might break even on that factor, though, and then all of your ad dollars can go to meeting production expenses.

Sales techniques

The beauty of having a smaller publication is that if you see an opening for advertising dollars in an area that you hadn't considered before, you can always slant the publication a little in the right direction to appeal to that market and take in some additional ad revenue. It's always possible to put out special issues relating to an advertiser market. Be cautious, though, not to make it look like a puff sheet, filled only with materials about the advertisers on the subsequent pages, or your credibility will suffer.

Many smaller magazines are often in the bind of not having capital up front to pay a salaried-plus-commission sales rep, but the publisher doesn't really know anything about advertising sales. Selling advertising is an art. The one thing you will have in your favor is that you will know your product better than anyone else. It's your magazine and it will be your enthusiasm that will carry the publication over the long, lean months before your accounts receivable start building up.

If anyone can convince another person that your publication is worth a try, it will be you. You'll know the ins and outs of the magazine and what it offers that others of a similar type don't. You'll be the one who will know everything that is happening in coming months and what issue would be a good one in which to test an ad. Your lack of selling expertise will be made up for by your overabundance of enthusiasm.

Affording a good advertising space rep is one thing and finding a good rep is another thing entirely. You need someone who not only can present your product, but can, in fact, sell it. Most salespeople only deliver a message. They are not skilled in the art of selling a person on something that is more than what the person had been considering. This approach takes skill and training.

Anyone who walks into a potential advertiser's office and immediately reaches into a briefcase and recites a monologue about the demographics, circulation, and rates of the publication without even questioning the potential advertiser about what he needs from a magazine is a poor salesman. A rep should be supplied with background information such as where a company spends its money, how much is spent, and what market that company is trying to reach. Talk to the person you are trying to sell and find out why he hasn't tried another market and what has worked in past years. Listen to what he is saying to you. Most salespeople do not plan in advance and have no special approach when going in cold.

You cannot sell anything to people unless they feel they need or want the specific item. This doesn't take persuasion; it takes a carefully planned strategy. A sales rep has to involve the potential advertiser in the conversation. Dig; find out what the client wants and needs and then make that your main selling point. Tell him what he wants to know, not what you want to tell him.

Don't ever knock your competition. Compare the differences, and show how your publication can do a better job in specific areas; but never should one negative word be said about your fellow magazine publisher. Point out why advertising in your publication not only will save dollars but also will reach a new potential buying market. Always emphasize savings if it applies; and if it doesn't, emphasize the quality of the market that you reach even with a segmented audience.

Be ready for objections, too. Think up an answer to every possible objection: your rates are too high; we've never heard about you before; our ad budget is shot for this year; we use television only; we use word-of-mouth only; you don't have the right type of editorial matter for our company; we don't have an ad made up now; we like what we are already using.

Don't tell the potential advertiser that he is a jerk for thinking that way, but suggest concrete reasons for considering an ad in your magazine.

If research has been done correctly, it can be used to help fish out what a company really wants from its marketing campaign. Be certain that all key people at the company and its ad agency are on the comp (complimentary) mailing list.

Find out from secretaries and switchboard operators when is the best time to make appointments. If your contact is always hurried in the mornings or if he likes to leave at 3 p.m. each afternoon, don't make the appointment for 2:45 p.m. or another inconvenient time and expect the potential advertiser to give you all of his attention.

Read up on everything in the industry trade newspapers and magazines so you'll be on top of what is going on and know exactly what position your potential advertiser takes.

When you go in, you should be loaded with questions and insights to give you the upper hand when the conversation seems to be going the wrong way. Change the topic and get the advertiser talking about something important to him, not a fist full of statistics. Ask him about his marketing problems and what his sales goals are. Find out what demographic market he is trying to reach.

Question the advertiser about the thrust of his advertising campaign. Does he do mostly television and radio or major newspapers? If he feels television is his major market, has he ever considered combining it with print to give a media mix? Suggest potential solutions to problems that he might have been thinking about. When you are in his office, you should be carrying on a conversation. This means an exchange of ideas, not a recitation and one-sided dialogue.

When setting up an appointment, make sure that you are talking to the person who can make the final decision. Too often, time is wasted talking with someone who doesn't have any authority to give the final go-ahead. Get directly to this person so that you can answer any questions that he has. This is the person you have to convince, not some account executive who is only going to relay the message.

Once you do get into the office of this person, you had better have something important to say. Don't just tell him how good your magazine is. Apply all your knowledge to relate to his marketing objectives. Show him how you can benefit him in pursuit of his goals, how you can help him reach his target.

It is necessary to make this person feel that he is very important to you, that you respect his position of authority. Always have something to give to him that you have prepared—a chart, a competing ad of his that you can run for less and still reach the same market, or a news clipping about something that has just happened concerning his company. Let the potential advertiser know that you have taken the time to do some homework and that you didn't just walk in off the street on a whim after lunch.

If he hasn't advertised in your magazine, find out why he hasn't. Ask him point-blank, or you'll never find out. Be direct and he'll be honest with you in return. Perhaps it is because someone never returned a phone call and it was taken as an insult, or something equally petty. Or maybe the advertiser thinks that you slighted him by mentioning a competitor and not his company in the new products section of your magazine. Find out what the problem is—it might be easy to resolve.

With expenses getting higher and higher, it is not always economically feasible to be making business trips to all of your clients. To conserve fuel and your limited dollars, learn to write a good business letter. This can save you time and money, and it is a good way to keep lines of communication open.

Few people know how to write an effective letter. Each letter should be tailored to the person to whom you are writing. There is nothing as insulting as a letter that sounds as if it could have been written to anyone on the street corner.

Never start a letter by saying, "Enclosed is the information that you requested." It sounds like just another form letter and doesn't have any interest for the reader. Make all letters seem of a personal nature to the person whom you are addressing.

Something more to the effect of "After talking with you today, I found out some surprising results" will have much more impact than the other approach. Keep things on a one-to-one basis. It is a good idea to make a call beforehand, even if it is long distance, to establish a personal relationship with your client. This way your letter won't come in cold with ten others.

You should learn good letter writing as well as proper form, style, and business letter terminology.

Another point worth mentioning is the call report. Even a small magazine should design some form for reporting all calls that are made to potential advertisers. The practice is mandatory in a bigger sales operation and enables management to keep track of what is happening with the market area of each salesperson. The smaller publisher sometimes overlooks this seemingly unnecessary procedure.

Even if you have only one or two sales reps and are in constant contact with them throughout the day, it will still be worthwhile to record calls made to clients. In the beginning this might seem like a waste of time, but as your publication grows and more advertisers are added, it will be confusing trying to remember who was called when and what he said the last time you talked with him.

Even if only one call is made during an average day, the number will still mount up to a lot of calls to keep track of throughout the year.

Some advertisers will want you to call back in two weeks to remind them about a deadline. Some will want you to call about a certain issue coming up. Some might have been entirely against your publication when contacted. If you have a record of what the conversation was about, then the next time you call, you will know what angle to take when approaching the advertiser. Again, the approach should be on a personal level—and how can you be personal if you've forgotten what transpired on the last call?

Also record what letters and correspondence have been sent to the advertiser so you can check to see if he has received everything that he needs. This will give you an accurate record of all work that has been done over the past months and years. The telephone should never replace personal visits to clients. This should be used in conjunction and as reinforcement.

The old line that the budget is already closed for the year is, more times than not, only a way to get you out of the office. Any smart businessman will always jump at the chance to make money. Even if funds have already been scheduled elsewhere, there is always the possibility of expanding the budget or shifting the monies around.

Learn to detect when a negative answer is really the truth and when it is being used as a push out the door. And if a person says no, do a follow-up with either a call or a letter to make some other points that you wanted to call to his attention or that you had only recently found out yourself. Always help to keep the potential advertiser informed and up to date on what is happening.

The hardest part of making an advertising space call is the closing. Each salesperson has his own way of closing the sale, his own sense of timing as to the exact moment to get a commitment. Bring together all the points that you have been talking about and summarize them, point out the positives.

Be positive; don't hesitate, but simply ask the contact if he likes what you have been saying and agrees that your publication is better than he realized. Don't just say, "Can I expect an ad from you then?" Say something like "The closing date for our next issue is February 23. If that doesn't give you enough time to have materials to us, perhaps I can extend it a few days longer. Do you think that will be necessary?"

Put the client in a positive frame of mind; let him know that you are in control and know what you are doing. Let him have faith in you and in the magazine that you represent.

Prepare the sale in your mind from start to finish just in case the contact doesn't offer you any feedback. There is nothing worse than sitting across the desk from someone and having your mind go blank. By doing your homework, you can have issues that would be of special interest to your contact, especially any issues in which the contact's company has been mentioned. Or pull out issues in which his competition has advertised. Don't point it out, but be subtle and let the client realize for himself.

And don't ever go into an office with the attitude that you really need to sell an ad today. Don't let the potential advertiser think that he is doing you a favor by giving you an ad. The approach that your publication is the best thing that ever happened for this company, will work better than the "We really need your business" routine. Of course you need his business, and you both know it (and don't ever forget it, either), but make the client believe in your product. Make him realize that he needs you—not just that you need him. Show the client how special your magazine is and how he is going to benefit from advertising with you.

Selling space is not like selling a tangible item that you can hold in your hand. A space rep has to convey the quality of the magazine through his own personality and appearance. Someone with the get-tough attitude just won't make it selling for a new publication. You'll need someone who can build a strong working relationship and create a bond of confidence.

Perhaps it is not always possible to close a sale on the first office visit, but that doesn't mean that the call has been for nothing. It is one part of cultivating a working arrangement.

Making one sale is not as important as making a series of sales that will continue over the following months, and it takes time to show a potential advertiser that he is making the right decision.

A good space rep has to be intelligent enough to sense out what the contact is hesitant about and to answer these questions (even though they haven't been asked yet).

Just as important as bringing in new business is the task of servicing existing accounts. That means keeping the advertiser happy and seeing that all of his needs are taken care of. Making certain that his ad is in on time or that he knows when something special is happening is just as important as getting the advertiser interested in the first place. Once he's signed on the dotted line, it doesn't necessarily mean that you've got the ad in your pocket for good. If the advertiser misses the deadline or you forget to put his ad in, then you can't bill him. And that means a considerable loss of money as well as credibility.

The publisher of a smaller magazine might consider using sales reps. These are people employed by a firm to represent many publications at the same time. They usually represent between 5 and 20 publications and can, in fact, sell each publication to a contact who might be interested in more than one vehicle for getting his message across.

There are pros and cons for using sales reps. First of all, they take a cool 15 to 20 percent off the top of the page rate for commission; but if they are bringing in 20 pages of advertising per issue, what does that matter? Then again, some publishers of smaller magazines say that they do not get the coverage from reps that they should.

You as publisher will have to weigh the value of using reps. Determine the number of full-time reps that a firm uses, what territory they cover, and what other publications they handle. You must realize that a sales rep will never be as excited about your magazine as you are, but you'll want to make certain that the people handling your publication are well suited to answer questions about your magazine. If you have a technical publication, you won't want a rep who doesn't understand the mechanics of your scope. But you do want someone who can sell; and sales reps work only on commission, which means that they have to sell or they don't make any money. This is an incentive in itself.

Many times rep firms won't want to take on a smaller publication because its low sales volume isn't going to bring in enough profit. If a rep firm does see a potential for increased volume over the coming years, it may put in the time to develop the business. This is usually done if there is a common trust and the firm knows that the publisher isn't going to drop its rep after the contacts have been made.

If both parties are fair and intelligent about the situation, a working arrangement can be made that could bring years of high sales profit. Many times, though, the new magazine publisher can't afford to give the 20-percent commission away when every dollar counts.

If you decide to handle ad sales yourself, you may be able to use some random tips on selling ads:

- Whenever possible, try to call on both the ad agency and its client. In some cases, the client relies almost completely on the recommendations of the agency for media buys. In other cases, the agency simply places a budget which is totally dictated by the client company. In most cases, however, there is a good deal of discussion and debate over just how the ad budget will be structured. If you have called on both agency and client company, you have covered all the bases and your chances of having your magazine included in the company's ad budget are greatly increased.
- Generally, the larger the company, the farther in advance is the finalization of its ad budget. In many cases, ad budgets are prepared as far as a year in advance. That means you must make your pitch before the budget is finalized or miss out for an entire year.

The secret is to simply ask the agency when the budget planning takes place and then make sure you get to them in time with your media kit and sales calls.

- Occasionally, you make an ad call in which the contact will simply act in a rude manner, either with hostile comments and questions, or by letting you sit in the lobby even though you had an appointment.

Our advice is to shrug off the rude comment or two; but if they persist, let your contact know you don't appreciate them. Chances are you'll catch him off guard and put him in a subordinate position with you in control of the meeting.

As for sitting in lobbies, don't wait for more than ten minutes. Instruct the receptionist to page your contact again. If he doesn't greet you, jot a brief note on a business card and leave. Call in a day or two and make another appointment. Next time, you'll find your contact will go out of his way to be cordial.

Remember, you are seeing the contact because you have information which will help him or his client make money. If you allow yourself to be denigrated, your chances of closing a sale will be greatly lessened.

Sales tools

There are two primary ad sales tools—the ad rate card and the so-called media kit. You will need both to sell your magazine effectively.

The rate card

The rate card can be a simple card or piece of paper, but more often, it is a pamphlet or booklet, varying in size from two to a dozen or more pages. The complexity of the rate card will depend on the complexity of your magazine—if you have various editions and regional ad rates, your rate card will be quite complex.

But every rate card, whether simple or complex, should contain the following essentials:

• List of closing dates (ad deadlines) and dates of publication for an entire calendar year or season.

• List of all ad sizes, giving exact dimensions for each.

• List of all rates, including those for all sizes of ads and

special frequency rates (low rates for running in three, six, or other specified number of issues during the season or year).
- Important mechanical requirements, such as type of halftones and other ad materials (camera-ready copy, film, Scotch prints, and so on).
- Other important information, such as agency commission (if any is allowed), terms for payment, short-rate policy, and positioning requirements.
- Last but perhaps most important of all, be sure to include your magazine's mailing address and phone number. You will be amazed at how many ad agencies will call or write with questions, problems, and proposals.

If you are unfamiliar with how to design your magazine's rate card, the best bet is to obtain rate cards from five or six other magazines and study them. Also, check with your printer and typesetter to determine their special requirements. If your printer needs ad negatives which are right-reading and emulsion side down, and your advertisers send negatives which are left-reading or emulsion side up, you've got big troubles.

And when you get those other rate cards to study, make sure you learn all the terminology in each one of them so that you can answer advertisers' questions intelligently and can converse with your typesetter and printer in their own language.

Finally, be sure your rate card contains a publisher's copy protective clause which indicates that advertisers and ad agencies assume all liability for the content of the ads they place. Try to check out all questionable ad claims anyway, and if an ad seems devious or dishonest, reject it. Not only will you prevent possible legal hassles with readers from occurring, but you'll also avoid potential threats to your magazine's integrity.

The media kit

The media kit is a sales package which is prepared by magazines and other publications and sent or hand-delivered to ad agencies and ad managers at potential advertiser companies.

Media kits range from a few simple sheets of information and

How to start your own magazine

EFFECTIVE DATE—SEPT. 1, 1978

Issue	Press Date	Ad Closing Date
(for 1978-79 ski season)		
Annual Trip Guide*	Sept. 1	Aug. 10
October Ski Show Issue	Sept. 22	Sept. 12
November Issue	Oct. 20	Oct. 10
December Issue	Nov. 24	Nov. 14
January Issue	Dec. 22	Dec. 12
February Issue	Jan. 25	Jan. 15
March Spring Skiing Issue	Feb. 16	Feb. 6

*See separate rate card for Guide.

TERMS: Payment due within 30 days after billing date. 1½% interest per month added to overdue accounts. Cash with order for accounts not settled within 60 days.

AGENCY COMMISSION: 15% of gross billing allowed **only** to recognized agencies on space, color and position provided account is paid within 30 days from invoice date.

SHORT RATES: Advertisers will be short-rated if, within a 6-month period from the date of the first insertion on their contract, they do not use the number of insertions upon which their billing has been based.

MECHANICAL REQUIREMENTS: Camera-ready artwork or 85-line screen negatives, right reading, emulsion down. Half tone PMTs should carry 10% dot in highlight, 20% in shadow. We can also prepare ads for advertisers. Cost of typesetting borne by advertiser or agency. Proofs furnished on request.

ADVERTISING RATES

Tabloid Page Units

	1 time	3 time	6 time
Full page (50 column inches)	$905	$795	$670
3/4 page (37½ column inches)	$720	$625	$530
1/2 page (25 column inches)	$580	$510	$440
1/4 page (12½ column inches)	$340	$300	$260
1/8 page (6¼ column inches)	$195	$170	$155

Standard Magazine Page Units

	1 time	3 time	6 time
Standard magazine page (30 column inches)	$640	$570	$490
1/2 Standard magazine page (20 column inches)	$490	$430	$380
1/2 Standard magazine page (15 column inches)	$390	$350	$310
1/3 Standard magazine page (10 column inches)	$275	$230	$210
1 column inch	$35		

A typical rate card

MULTIPLE UNITS of space in one issue are charged for at individual rates and are counted as individual units for the purpose of determining frequency discount. No bulk rates.

POSITION: Add 10% for specified position. Publisher reserves right to reposition ads according to space requirements.

COLOR: Spot color and full color available. Add 20% for second color, 40% for second and third colors, and 60% for four-color ads.

BLEEDS or oversize ads not available.

SPREADS: Spread advertisements are charged for at a rate of each individual unit on each facing page and count as two insertions.

PUBLISHER'S PROTECTIVE CLAUSE: Advertisers and advertising agencies assume liability for all content (including text, representation and illustrations) of advertisements printed, and also assume responsibility for any claims arising therefrom against the publisher.

AD SIZES

Tabloid Page Units

	Width	Depth
Full Page	10	12½
3/4 page	10	9¼
3/4 page	7¼	12½
1/2 page (vert)	4¾	12½
1/2 page (hor)	10	6¼
1/4 page	2¼	12½
1/4 page (vert)	4¾	6¼
1/4 page (hor)	10	3¼
1/8 page (vert)	2¼	6¼
1/8 page (hor)	4¾	3¼

Standard Magazine Units

	Width	Depth
Full mag. page	7¼	10
2/3 mag. page	4¾	10
1/2 mag. page (hor)	7¼	5
1/2 mag. page (vert)	4¾	7½
1/3 mag. page (vert)	2¼	10
1/3 mag. page (sq)	4¾	5
1/6 mag. page (vert)	2¼	5
1/6 mag. page (hor)	4¾	2¼

a rate card to elaborate creations containing charts, graphs, sample issues of the publication, detailed demographic surveys, feature story schedules, and comparisons of rates with those of other publications in the field.

What your media kit will look like will depend on how much money you can afford to spend, plus the amount of time you are willing to spend in gathering information of all types.

We suggest you obtain the media kits of five or six other magazines for study (just as you obtained the rate cards). Decide which features of each you want to include in your own kit and which you can do without. Just remember that providing too much information can be as harmful as too little. After all, few ad executives have the time or inclination to wade through miles of facts and figures to determine if they should advertise in a brand-new publication.

The trick is to design your media packet so that it can be dissected easily and quickly. And your media kit should reflect your magazine. If you are selling a super-slick product which appeals to the Mercedes Benz and country-club crowd, your media kit should be expensive-looking. On the other hand, if you publish a tabloid on newsprint, a too-slick media kit will cause the ad people to get suspicious about everything you say.

In the case of new magazines, you will essentially be citing potential circulation ad projections of planned growth. Elaborate demographic surveys at this point are silly. Wait until you establish a readership; then survey 500 or so subscribers to get a handle on whom your magazine is actually appealing to.

Few regionally circulated magazines or highly vertical magazines go in for elaborate demographic surveys, partly because of the prohibitive cost of hiring an outside firm to do a market study, and partly because it should be obvious to all just who your readers are (Michigan bird watchers, law students, or whoever).

Media kits can cost from two dollars or so up to as much as ten dollars apiece for materials and production costs. And this doesn't take into account the cost of having demographic surveys completed. Then there is the cost of mailing each media kit to the hundreds of people on your mailing list. You can see that the cost of producing this vital sales tool and getting it into the hands of decision makers can run to several thousand dollars at the minimum, and into six figures for nationally circulated magazines which are aiming at large circulation figures.

As an adjunct to your media kits, it is also essential that you get your magazine listed in the appropriate Standard Rate & Data Service (SRDS) directory. Many media buyers at ad agencies use SRDS publications as their chief guide to purchasing ad space, especially in specialized fields. Sometimes, you will receive an ad contract from an agency which you have never contacted, simply because of your listing in an SRDS publication. (For information on getting listed, write to Standard Rate & Data Service, 5201 Old Orchard Road, Skokie, Illinois 60076.)

10
Odds and ends

The purpose of this book is to provide the would-be publisher with specific, useful information in the planning, financing, and actual operation of a new magazine. We have covered the most important divisions of the publishing process chapter by chapter.

But there are still a number of important things which don't justify an entire chapter, yet bear mentioning nonetheless. And so, we have incorporated them into this final chapter, in no particular order of importance. They are: your own special logo; cover design; dealing with Uncle Sam; libel, slander, and other legal concerns; to copyright or not to copyright; and how much to charge.

Your own special logo

All businesses use logos as an instant means of identification, much the same way as the Roman legions all carried their own distinctive banners, and knights adorned shields and helmets with their coats of arms.

The trend in business today is toward nondescript, often bland corporate logos, from the NBC "N" to the "IBM" composed of horizontal lines for that corporation. But that doesn't mean you must or should follow suit in designing the logo for your magazine.

Keep in mind that if you are producing a consumer publication, it will be fighting for the attention of readers along with a hundred or more other magazines. If it doesn't jump out and practically bite the person, it won't get a second look. And even trade publications and others which do not rely on retail sales for circulation should be distinctive anyway. Most people, from businessmen to housewives, are deluged with all sorts of literature, from junk mail to magazines. You must catch their attention through a dynamic cover and draw them into reading your magazine, or it is apt to be tossed into a corner with the rest of the junk mail.

Once the reader becomes familiar with your magazine and learns that it is filled with interesting, provocative articles and photos, the mere sight of your own distinctive logo will be enough to ensure that your magazine will be read.

The way to ensure instant recognition of your magazine's logo is to settle on its basic look and then stick with it. For example, even from a distance, no one can confuse *Time* magazine's picture-frame border in red, with the cover of any other newsmagazine. Likewise, the covers of *National Geographic*, with its gilded, yellow border, are also instantly recognizable.

We're not saying you must go with this kind of border. In fact, such borders are generally considered archaic, compared to the uncluttered covers of magazines such as *Playboy*.

Cover design

There is no one right way to design a cover. You may elect to superimpose your logo over a full-color photo which bleeds off the cover on all four sides. You may use reverse type for your logo, with the cover photo floating in the center, so that the color acts as a plain border. You may go with a newspaper-style logo on top, with the photo beneath and "teaser" headlines to inside stories running down the left side, either double-burned (superimposed) on the photo, or by themselves.

The actual design of the cover is important, but equally important is the maintenance of a continuity in the "look" of your magazine's covers.

Regardless of the final appearance of your covers, they all should contain certain basic information, which should be repeated on a title page inside—retail price, volume and number of the issue, and date of publication. Teaser headlines are not essential, but they certainly will have a bearing on the retail sales of your magazine.

Placement of the logo is also important. Generally, the best place for the logo is at the top of the cover. The reason should be obvious—unless people can see the logo in the magazine rack, they won't buy it.

What about holding costs down for covers? The most obvious way is by using just one or two colors instead of a full four-color cover, but this can be self-defeating if your magazine depends on retail sales. Covers with only one color plus black just don't look as good as the four-color covers, and regardless of the quality of its contents, most people will automatically assume your magazine isn't as good as the one next to it in full color.

A better way to hold cover costs down is by avoiding the superimposition of various teaser headlines over your cover photo, since this can double or triple the cost of your color separations.

Another way to hold cover costs down is to offer covers to those who are willing to pick up the tab for the separation costs; but this can get touchy unless you maintain absolute control over the final cover. You also have to consider the possibly negative reaction on the part of competing businesses.

For example, if you publish a boating magazine and you use a cover photo with separations provided by Johnson Motors, will Evinrude and Mercury object because their motors weren't shown off the same way? In the case of advertisers, you can wind up losing far more in ad revenue than you save in production costs; so think long and hard before you make a decision one way or the other.

Dealing with Uncle Sam

As a magazine publisher, you will be dealing with the government in two main ways—as an income-producing business, and as a user of the United States mails.

The best way to avoid hassles over taxes is to hire a CPA (certified public accountant) rather than just an accountant, and to go with one who has experience in the publishing field. Publishing, just like many other businesses, has its own special tax rules (and loopholes) and a knowledgeable CPA can save you his fee many times over, not to mention keeping you out of hot water.

No matter how small your new magazine is (even if it is a one-man operation), we strongly advise you find the best CPA in your area to handle your business accounting.

As for dealing with the United States Postal Service, we should tell you right now that this is apt to be the most confusing, frustrating, and difficult of all the tasks facing you as publisher.

The United States Postal Service is a monopoly. Even worse, it has the power of the federal government behind it. No matter how large your magazine is, you will always be forced to approach the postal people with hat in hand, and that includes your dealings with the lowliest clerks.

Postal regulations are like army regulations. They are open to wide variation in interpretation, and what one local clerk may tell you is apt to be overruled by the next person down the line.

When we started our very first magazine, we heard all kinds of horror stories regarding dealing with the post office. So, to avoid any possible problems, we hired a first-rate mailing house to handle our circulation records, address and sort our publications and deliver them to the local post office.

Next, we paid the postmaster a call and spent several hours going over all the many requirements for mailing second class, which is the most inexpensive method of mailing magazines. We were told exactly what to print in our masthead pertaining to our pending second-class permit, where to have the mailing labels placed on the cover, and other requirements.

Odds and ends

We were ecstatic when 45,000 copies of our very first issue were delivered to the post office—that is, until a clerk refused to accept the magazines because they didn't bear a bulk mailing permit indicia.

The postmaster had incorrectly advised us regarding mailing while the second-class permit was pending, but when we went back to him, he denied telling us the indicia wasn't needed, obviously in fear that someone higher up would jump all over him.

The magazines sat on the loading dock of the post office for two weeks while we tried every avenue of appeal, all the way to Washington. Finally, in desperation, we had our mailing house retrieve all 45,000 copies and attach bulk mailing indicias on each by hand. The additional cost came to something over $2,000, not to mention the two-week delay.

In the years since then, we have run into similar problems with other publications, often getting four or five different rulings on a particular postal regulation.

Three years ago, frustrated publishers of magazines, newspapers, and other periodicals in the Greater Chicago area banded together to form the Chicago Area Publishers' Council on Mailing, which we promptly joined. To our surprise, we discovered that the kind of ongoing problems we faced with the postal authorities were not unique. Rather, we learned that publications from the smallest newsletters all the way to industry giants such as *Playboy* had similar problems.

Dealing with screwed-up regulations and running into hostile postal personnel are just two areas of concern. You will also find that the United States Postal Service is doing everything in its power to push second-class and controlled-circulation rates through the ceiling, in the belief that by increasing rates as much as tenfold over the next five years, they can solve their own budget problems.

What the Postal Service is actually going to do is to force a great many publishers out of business, and in the long run, their postal revenues will suffer. As for infringing on the First Amendment guarantee of free speech by forcing publishers out of business, that has yet to really hit the American people.

What this means to you as a publisher of a new magazine is that to ensure your existence in the years to come, you must determine right now how to meet the ever-increasing costs of mailing your magazine.

Some magazines will become much more vertical, limiting their readership to an ever more select few. Others will pass postage costs on through increased subscription rates, in the hope that readers won't simply drop their subscriptions. (The day of the $20 magazine subscription should arrive by 1984—an appropriate year, to be sure.)

Libel, slander, and other legal concerns

An understanding of the laws pertaining to libel, slander, and invasion of privacy are essential for you as a magazine publisher, and for your editorial staff as well. A single serious slip which results in a lawsuit can put you out of business. Even if you win the suit, the legal costs can be crippling.

The best rule to follow is when in doubt concerning anything which may be libelous, slanderous, or an invasion of privacy, don't print it—at least not until you consult with a lawyer who is an expert in the field.

Most metropolitan newspapers follow another guiding rule. Instead of withholding anything which may be libelous, slanderous, or an invasion of privacy, they withhold any item which they think they may be sued for printing. If the person in question is a wealthy man who is apt to take them into court, they defer. If the man is an itinerant worker with little or no money, they print it.

It's a hell of a way to run a railroad, we agree, but we speak from a dozen years in the newspaper and magazine publishing business.

An in-depth discussion of the laws pertaining to libel, slander, and invasion of privacy will not be attempted here, partly because it would take an entire volume, and also because the laws are constantly being rewritten and reinterpreted by various courts. Nonetheless, here are some things to keep in mind:

In order for an item to be libelous, it need not be incorrect, contrary to what most journalists believe. You may report a completely factual incident, but if the person whose name appears in print can prove the item caused him public embarrassment or damage to his reputation, he can sue and collect. Fortunately, few people bother, preferring to let the matter die.

Public figures are fair game for the press, and in order for them to sue and win for libel, they must show not only that your report was inaccurate, but also that your publication printed the item with malicious intent. Of course, the question of just who is categorized as a public figure is open to continuing debate. Usually, public figures include politicians, movie stars, professional athletes, and others of special fame or notoriety.

As for invasion of privacy, it is also a ticklish subject. Does a reporter who carries a hidden tape recorder into a bordello invade the privacy of the prostitute? Does the photographer who uses a telephoto lens to photograph a local politician taking money from a lobbyist in his own backyard invade the privacy of the politician?

If your publication is of such a nature that your staffers and free-lancers will be getting involved in such precarious situations, you had better make sure that: (a) you have plenty of liability insurance; (b) you have a good lawyer; and (c) you are ready to face the possibility of losing a very expensive lawsuit—one which could exceed the limits of your insurance.

Even if your magazine is not at all controversial, it is still a good idea to carry liability insurance, just in case you stumble onto a hot story which you elect to run, or in case one of your people simply makes a mistake which results in a lawsuit.

To copyright or not to copyright

The great majority of magazines seldom if ever bother to copyright articles which appear on their pages. Often, theirs is the lone publication in the field, so there is no need to protect the article from piracy.

And many other magazines which do have competition feel that copyrighting a story which they run first is silly, because if the opposition uses it after them, it is like admitting they were scooped.

Then, too, most articles in magazines are neither particularly timely nor controversial; so again a copyright simply isn't needed to protect the story from pilferage. Even if a story is copyrighted, there is nothing to stop a competing publication from using it as a basis for developing additional facts and then incorporating the material in different form for their own article.

Copyrights are most valuable when used to protect published fiction. In such cases, the copyright would include first and subsequent publication rights; stage, motion picture, and TV rights; and adaptation and translation rights.

Granted, there will be times when you want to protect a piece of nonfiction through a copyright, but the decision will be yours.

How long is a copyright good? It holds for the life of the author plus an additional 50 years—which is really protecting an article.

What is required to copyright an article? It is incredibly simple. All you have to do is print the required copyright notice (the symbol ©, the word "Copyright" or the abbreviation "Copr.") as well as the year of publication and name of the copyright proprietor on all copies.

If a regular staff member writes an article which you as publisher copyright, you own that article. If a free-lancer writes an article which you copyright, then in order for you to own that article after first publication you must get a written agreement from that writer stating that he sells you the first and all subsequent uses of the article.

Technically, for copyright protection you must "promptly" file a Claim to Copyright along with a six-dollar fee and two copies of the work. But in practice, you can file anytime and still protect the work, as long as it carried the required information listed above. In fact, there is one case on record in which the publisher filed for a copyright 27 years after the date of publication and the court ruled it was still a "prompt" filing.

The only drawbacks to not formally filing for copyrights are that (a) you can be subject to a fine from the Register of

Copyrights, and (b) you can't start a lawsuit for copyright infringement until you file.

So, if another publication uses your copyrighted article, and you want to file suit, you simply make your official filing and then proceed.

How much to charge

In mapping plans for your new magazine, the best advice we can give regarding both ad rates and subscription and retail sales is to start high. People are much less likely to complain if you come right at them from the start with high prices, than if you start low and then start jumping your prices rapidly because you miscalculated on costs.

High ad and cover prices not only will get you into the black quicker but will also add to the prestige of your publication. It is a well-known fact of psychology that people tend to equate price with quality. If Cadillac were to sell its new models for the same price as Volkswagens, people simply would not believe that Cadillac was a better automobile (and, more important, a more prestigious one). The same rationale applies to magazines.

The best way to determine ad rates is to figure your estimated total cost of operation, then estimate conservatively how much advertising you will carry in the coming year, and then fix your ad rates so that you realize a profit of at least 20 percent. If you hit or exceed that objective, great. If you don't, at least you will have a hedge of 20 percent before showing a loss.

The problem is that you can price yourself out of the game if your CPM (cost of a page of advertising per thousand copies you print) is too high. The best way to avoid this is to go through Standard Rate & Data Service's various publication directories and compare ad rates and circulation of other publications which appear to be similar in various ways to yours (type of audience, type of format, similar circulation).

As a brand-new publication, you will be selling promises of circulation, not actual circulation. Eventually, when you develop a strong, provable circulation base, then you should consider providing advertisers with an ABC (Audit Bureau of Circulation) report or BPA (Business Publications Audit of Circulation).

Such audited reports are supposed to weigh heavily with ad agencies; but unless your magazine is a high-volume, nationally circulated book, we suggest you simply provide a sworn statement of circulation to advertisers and thus eliminate a whole lot of expense and additional record keeping.

As for building circulation, it will all depend on the kind of magazine you are producing. If it is a consumer publication, then you must get retail distribution in the cities which you want to reach. If it is a specialized sports magazine, you may elect to establish your own distribution network—say, a bowling magazine which you send to bowling alleys, or a fishing magazine which you send to fishing resorts. Of course, then you have to keep track of returns and you also take on what can become a massive job of billing and collections.

One of the best ways for a new magazine to go is with a combination of paid and controlled (free) circulation. Gradually eliminate the free copies as you build paid circulation. Or simply make your publication one with a completely controlled circulation and gear your ad rates so that your profits are derived entirely from them.

To help you decide which way you should go, why not send a query to your list of potential advertisers. You may be surprised to learn that many aren't concerned whether each copy is paid for as long as it reaches the people they want to reach with their ad messages.

Some of the most successful controlled-circulation magazines are the trade journals, such as magazines for dentists, or welders, or librarians. The key is to find out who your advertisers want to reach and then go about reaching them.

Glossary of publishing terms

ABC: Audit Bureau of Circulation, the best known of several agencies which provide independent audits of subscribers and retail sales for publications of all types.
Ad rep: An independent agent who contracts to sell ad space for a number of publications on a commission basis.
Book: Printer's jargon for a magazine.
Caption: Printed information which accompanies a photo, explaining or identifying it.
Coated stock: Paper which has been treated with clay and other materials to provide a slick, coated surface.
Cold type: Type produced directly on paper by photographic means as opposed to hot type, which is a cast series of letters on a lead slug and produced by a Linotype machine.
Controlled circulation: Refers to a method of distribution which is free or mainly free. A controlled-circulation mailing permit provides one of the least costly methods of mailing magazines (compare **second-class mailing permit**).
Copyright: Registered ownership of the privilege of reproducing a story, poem, or other printed piece.
CPM: Cost per page of advertising per 1,000 copies of a magazine.

Cropping: Marking a photo so that a portion of it is eliminated during reproduction.

Dummy: A sheet which represents a magazine page and which bears instructions for pasteup of editorial material and ads; also, to make such a page.

Editorial: The department of a magazine which is responsible for all non-advertising content; also, the printed viewpoint or position of magazine management.

Four-color separation: Black, blue, red, and yellow primary components of a color photo or transparency separated into individual pieces of film (either positive or negative).

Free-lancer: A writer or photographer who is an independent agent, paid by individual assignment.

Galley: Copy of articles to be used for proofreading and dummying.

Gravure: A method of printing often used for press runs of one million or more copies.

Gutter: Margin between the inside column of a magazine page and the fold.

Head: Short for headline.

Head shot: A photo which shows just a person's head and shoulders.

Hot type: Cast lines of type characters on lead slugs (compare **cold type**).

In-house: Work handled by a magazine's staff instead of an outside agency or shop.

Letterpress: Printing method using cast lead plates; slowly being phased out but still economical for some applications.

Libel: Defamatory statements published about an individual, usually not true, or not justified.

Logo: The special insignia of a company. In the case of magazines, the logo usually appears at the top of the front cover, on the title page, and atop the masthead.

Masthead: Statement of ownership of a magazine which also usually lists key staffers. The masthead normally appears within the first five pages because of post regulations.

Media kit: A packet usually containing such items as rate card, demographic information, and sample issue; designed to assist advertisers in determining whether to purchase ad space.

Newsprint: Paper made from wood pulp and used in newspapers and some tabloid magazines.

Offset stock: A type of paper which is much whiter and more substantial than newsprint but less costly than most coated stock.

Outquote: A quotation taken from the text of an article and reprinted, usually in larger type and set off by white space or rules.

Pica: A unit of measure used by printers. Six picas equal an inch.

Point: A unit of measure used by printers. Twelve points equal a pica.

Pro forma: A business plan which includes details of anticipated expenses and revenue; used to borrow funds from banks and to interest potential investors.

Proof: Copy of an article, photo, or magazine page; used to check for errors prior to printing.

Rate card: A sheet or booklet which contains advertising rates, sizes, publication dates, closing dates, and mechanical requirements for ads.

Second-class mailing permit: Granted by the United States Postal Service to publications with more than 50 percent paid circulation; provides least costly method of mailing magazines.

Standing head: A column headline which remains the same from issue to issue.

Tabloid: A format for newspapers and magazines. Standard tabloid trim size is 11½ inches wide by 14 inches deep.

Trim size: The physical size of a page after it comes off the press.

Web press: Type of press used for offset printing; most efficient for press runs of a few thousand to about a million copies.

Index

A

Accountant. *See* CPA
Advance planning, 23–24
Advertisers, 7–8, 17, 23, 52
   advertisement layout, 27, 41
   call report, 83–84
   list, 9–11
   media kit, 91–93
   rate card, 90–91, *illus.* 86–87
   rates, 12, 24, 60, 63, 103
   revenues, 4, 60–62, 63–64, 73
   selling space, 79–91
Advertising Age, 28
Annual Skisport Vacation Guide, 6
AP stylebook, 41–42
Art Waxer III, 44
Audit Bureau of Circulation
   (ABC), 70, 104, 105

B

Boards, 42, *illus.* 43

Book, 7
Budgeting, 59–61, 63–67
Business Publications Audit of
   Circulation (BPA), 104

C

Captions, 34, 35, 40
Chicago Area Publishers' Council
   on Mailing, 99
Chicago Daily News, 6, 26
Chicago Football Weekly, 7
Chicago Today, 6
Circulation, 4, 69–74, 104
Cold type, 42–44
Collection, 61–63
Columnists, 18
Column width, 35, 38
Competition, 4, 18, 73, 76, 81
Compugraphic, 46, 47
Content, 17–24, 26, 74
Controlled circulation, 104
Copier, 66

109

Index

Copy block, 35
Copy editing, 41–42
Copyrights, 101–3
Costs, operating, 4, 48–49, 59–67
   budgeting, 59–61, 63–67
   pasteup, 44
   printing, 57
   typesetting, 46–47
CountryStyle, 28
Cover, 51–52, 96–97
CPA, 13, 98
CPM, 103
Cropping photographs, 32
Customer service, 72–73
Cutlines, 34, 35, 40

D

Deadlines, 20, 21, 22–23
Demographic surveys, 74, 92
Digest format, 26, 27
Dummy, 37–41, *illus.* 38

E

Editorial policy, 19
Editorials, 18
Executive editor, 19–20
Experience, 4, 41

F

Feature articles, 17–18
Field, Marhsall V, 6
Format, 26–28
Fringe benefits, 3, 4
Futura, 31

G

Gravure, 55
Grid sheets, 42, *illus.* 43

H

Hang Gliding, 8
Headlines, 34, 40
Hefner, Hugh, 1
Helvetica, 31
Hobie Hot Line, 7
Hollister, Lloyd, 5
"Horizontal makeup," 25
Hot type, 44

I

IBM typewriter, 66
Invasion of privacy, 100–1
Investors, 15–16

J

"Jump line" designation, 40

L

Layout, 24–26, 31, 34, 40
Letterpress, 54
Letter writing, 83
Libel, 100–1
Life, 6
"Live matter," 27, 38
Loans, 9, 11–15
Logo, 95–96

M

Mailing. *See* Postal Service, U.S.
"Make-good" ad, 61
Managing editor, 19–20
Media kit, 64, 91–93
Mergenthaler, 46
Mock-up issue, 11–12
"Modular layout," 25
Ms., 8

N

National Geographic, 96
Negatives, 48–49
"News hole," 41
Newspaper publishing, 6
News stories, 17

O

Office equipment, 66–67
Offset, 54
"Open pages," 41

P

Page dummy, 37–41, *illus.* 38
Pages, number of, 52
Page spread lineup, 52
Paper, 4, 51, 57
Pasteup, 39–40, 42–45
   costs, 44
People, 18, 34
Photographs, 27, 32–34, 35, 40
Phototypesetting, 42–44
PI advertisement, 71
Plates, 49
Playboy, 1, 96
Postage costs, 4, 65, 99, 100
Postal Service, U.S., 55, 98–100
Post office box, 65
Press credentials, 3
Press releases, 76–77
Press runs, 51–52
Price per issue, 73, 103–4
Printer, 21, 22, 27, 28, 42, 49–52, 53–54, 55–58
   bids, 54, 57
   costs, 57
Printing methods, 54–55
Printing "rep," 50
Production, 21, 37–52

Pro forma, 11, 12–13, 14, 15

R

Rate card, 90–91, *illus.* 86–87
Reader, The, 5
Reporters, 2
Rolling Stone, 28

S

Sales promotion, 75–78
Sales reps, 88–89
Sans serif typefaces, 31
Scheduling, 21–22, 23–24
Screened stats, 48–49
Serif typefaces, 28, 31
Skisport, 5–6
Slander, 100–1
Slug, 40
Smith-Corona typewriter, 66
Sources, reporter's, 2
Sports publications, 7
Standard magazine format, 27
Standard Rate & Data Service, 10, 93, 103
   Advertiser Book, 10
   consumer magazine directory, 8–9
   Red Book, 10
Standing head, 18
Stationary, business, 10–11, 65–66
Stock, 15
Stripping, 48–49
Stylebook, 41–42
Subscription rates, 73, 103–4
Subscription sales, 4, 69–74, 104

T

Tabloid format, 27–28
Tax loopholes, 4

Index

Telephone answering service, 66–67
Telephone bills, 64, 65
Time, 96
Trade shows, 77–78
Travel, 3
Typesetting, 21, 42, 45–48
   costs, 46–47
Typewriters, 66
Typography, 25, 26, 28–31, 34–35
   typefaces, *examples,* 29–30

U–V

Vertical books, 7, 73

W

Watergate, 2
Waxing machine, 44
Winnetka Talk, 5
Women's liberation movement, 8
WomenSport, 8
Writing, 19–20